THE
Bridge
HAS NO
Railings

The
Bragde
Has No
Railings

October 2015

For Shirley~
with gratitude
for your
support and
encouragement~
Betty

Elizabeth Bourque Johnson

Mill City Press • Minneapolis

Mill City Press, Inc.
322 First Avenue N, 5th floor
Minneapolis, MN 55401
612.455.2293
www.millcitypublishing.com

ISBN-13: 978-1-63413-710-2
LCCN: 2015913205

Cover Design by Colleen Rollins
Typeset by Mary K. Ross

www.bridgehasnorailings.com

Printed in the United States of America

For
Kristin, Stephanie, Patricia, and Julie

and for Bob

CONTENTS

Introduction   xiii

PART ONE   1

I.   A Certain Day   3

Destination   5
Standing by the Coffin, You Console Me   8
From Room to Room   9
Can You See   10
Superior, the Day the Ice Broke Up   11
Did You Know   12
The Groundskeepers   13
The Woman Who Wailed   14
Dies Irae   15
Your First Birthday after Death   16
Imperative   17
You Come Back   18
Proceedings   19
Her Grave Is on a Hill   21
Survivor   23
Aldebaran   25
If You Walk with Me   27
Now   28

II. God's Hands   29

God's Hands Look So Busy from Here   31
The Year the Cherries Were So Good   33
Without Peril   35
In the Shadow of My House   36
Always   38
Something New   40
Strawberries   41
Going over the Bridge   43
Homestead Avenue   44
First Kiss   45
We Come Home   46
His Mother Talks at Dinner   47
What a Child Must Carry   48
Twelve-and-a-Half   50
Flight from Detroit   51
Three Teeth in a Brown Envelope   52
Under This Broken Sky   53
Halley Watch, 1986   54
To Pablo Neruda,
    from His Mother, with Love   56
Daughter of Kinetic Air   59
Geography Lesson   60
Stephanie's Wolves   63
She Invites Me to the Mountains   64
What My Father Said   65
Past Pictures   67
Prayer for Children   68

III. Something   69

    What Holds   71
    Loons for Life   72
    Two Chairs and an Umbrella Table   73
    Hunger   74
    the edge of loneliness   76
    No Language for This   77
    After You Left, I   78
    The String of Betrayal Plucked   79
    Something   80
    What He Said When I Asked Why   81
    Everything Is Experiment   82
    A Woman Sitting on a Rock   84

        PART TWO   87
IV. Enough   89

    No Ordinary Tree   91
    Go into the Desert   92
    Enough   93
    The Women   94
    The Figure of History   96
    Sea Gull   98
    Shakespeare's Daughters   100
    In the Marble Rotunda, by a Fountain   103
    A Forest   105
    Snow and Silence   107
    An Osprey   108

Absence   111

One Prayer   112

Nana, Steadfast   114

Lament at Low Tide   115

This Is a Woman's House   118

Stars: A Gift   120

Bitter in My Mouth   122

Survivors   124

What Jackie Said   125

Godson by Proxy   126

The Plagues, the Ghosts   127

For My Brother, Never Dying   128

The Palms   129

Snowflakes   130

V. Sing Anyway   131

Alone on Sunset Rock   133

The Question Is Safety   135

She Thinks She Is a River   136

November, All Souls   137

I Sing Anyway   138

How to Be Alone   139

Glaciers and Women   140

The *Mesabi Miner* Appears on
   Lake Superior   141

Cold November Morning   142

Though Stuck in Traffic,
   I Am Never without Poetry   143

In the Hotel Bar   144

Change We Need 146

In the Time of the Cherry Blossoms 147

Paris 149

American Memorial 150

November Gale, Lake Superior 151

Poem of Wonder 152

Worry 153

A Secret 154

Screen Saver 156

look no further over my life 157

Paint Me 158

Gloria Mundi 159

VI. Everything Beautiful 161

Beach Walk at Happy Hour 163

Periwinkles 164

Faith 166

Waiting for Love 168

Pinecliff Woman Saves Dog 170

The Table 171

The Babies Tell Us 172

Bob and the Graves 173

Prophecies 174

Bob in the Garden 175

New England Poem 176

To Leap Overboard with Auden 180

A Meditation on Retirement:

  My Daughter Worries I'll Be Bored 181

My Poem to the Prairie 182

Portrait of Grace at Nine, Lake Superior   184

As You Are Forty   185

The Lupines along Highway 61   186

Facebook Post from Tricia   187

The Telephone   189

Rogue River Run   190

Clean Your Closets Now, She Said   191

What We Leave Behind   192

As Long as We Don't Fight It   193

A Childhood   194

Solstice Season   197

Ascent, Descent, No Middle Ground   198

INTRODUCTION

When the call came on a cold afternoon that Kristin had been severely injured in a car accident, her father and I flew to Chicago, where friends met us and drove us to South Bend. I had with me a notebook because I thought she would be in the hospital for a while and I would need to take notes, as well as write down questions for the doctors. I didn't have time for notes; she was dead by morning.

In my notebook I recorded the coroner's information, flight times, and other details about getting her back to Minneapolis with us the next day. Then I wrote down the awful words that she was gone.

Some days later, as the younger children returned to school, the house settled into emptiness. I opened the notebook and started writing. I wrote every day. You can imagine the tears and anger on those pages. Months later, in a class at the Loft, a teacher's comment took me by surprise: "What you are writing are poems." Who, me?

I kept writing, and some of it was poems, but mostly it was a way for me to express the anger, fear, and sorrow of those days, months, and years. Gradually the horror left my body, taking up residence on a page where I could twist it and turn it and figure out how to live with it. Loss doesn't disappear. But everyone who is deeply hurt by loss has to find a way to live with that loss, to find a safe place for it, and to become stronger than it is. Poetry, to my great surprise, was my way. Poetry grasps the huge and ungovernable and funnels it down into language that can contain it.

It's thirty years since that time, and I've written almost every day. It feels right this year to collect the poems I want to save as a remembrance of the loss and the healing and the amazing power of writing.

Friends were amazing, too. So many came to our house with roasts and stews and fruit and flowers and brownies—I wish I could remember who brought eight dozen dinner rolls—and they stayed beside us in individual ways for months and months until we could walk alone. Debbie Ducar walked me around the neighborhood every night for at least the first year, listening. Bridge group, book group, gourmet group all circled around. Our extended families, though loving, were far away; our friends became our family, and it is so to this day.

Writing and poetry became my joy and my work. I am grateful to the talented and large-hearted teachers who guided me: Richard Solly, Patricia Hampl, Michael Dennis Browne, and Deborah Keenan in particular. I appreciate, as well, my mentors and friends in the doctoral program at the University of Minnesota, especially Shirley Nelson Garner and the late Kent Bales.

Steadfast love and gratitude to each of you who has walked with me. You inhabit these poems.

Elizabeth Bourque Johnson

A certain day became a presence to me:
                    . . . it leaned over
and struck my shoulder as if with
the flat of a sword . . .

PART ONE

I. A Certain Day

DESTINATION

after Margurite Duras

In the plane I am like a sleepwalker. My hands clench in my lap. I look at no one, not the stewardess, the passengers. They have their destinations. A day ago I would have wondered about them. Now I don't wonder at all. I've stopped knowing about others. I am no longer a part of them, nor they of me. I am only myself, the mother.

I fly through night on this plane. It is only for me. My transit is what matters. Get there in time. Before anyone else makes decisions. That is for me; everyone knows that is for me.

South Bend, that's where she is. By ambulance from Plymouth, Indiana. The side of the road in the snow, heart stopped, blow to the head, not dying, not. Resuscitated, IV started, lifted by the paramedic. It's cold in Indiana.

Storm off the lake, wild wind and snow. The phone call: Marshall County Sheriff's Office. What happened? Tell me. "You'll have to talk to the doctor, ma'am." Her mouth is half open. "Hold, please." She calls out for her mother. I can't breathe on hold. Pain bursts through my face.

Far too many people on the airplane. I need wings of my own. She is calling my name. On all the roads of America people die, girls like her. Thousands, tens of thousands. Not her. She is at once one of thousands and, for me, completely separate and distinct.

I know all one can know when one knows nothing. They pull her out of the car, then all over her body for lungs, for heart. Clinical eyes focus on my daughter. Even without breath she calls me, *Mother*. What other name could she utter? Those with other names have nothing in common with me.

People all over O'Hare are laughing, especially those reunited. It was suppertime, I came in with groceries, the phone rang. Now it's night in Chicago, far yet to drive. She's in ICU. What have they done to her?

Friends meet us with their car. I can't talk to them. I'm drawn to a point, all senses. At Christmas she said, "College is a start to my life." The crash. In the snow by the side of the road. The ambulance, the ER, trauma center. Separated by this large night.

Nothing in the world belongs to me now except this child in a white bed. It's a black night. The end of the world. My death wouldn't hurt anyone. Just a simple death. I shall merely have died. It's a matter of indifference to me.

When I die, she can live, they can all go on. I'll tell them, "I can die this time. You will all be fine." I'll be clever and die in this car as we ride, then she can climb in and go home. It's all I can do. They may be waiting for me. *Pull the plug?* No. But then she would live as dust, as Karen Ann Quinlan dust. They say, *Pull the plug?* Can I say Yes? No?

I ride in the back seat of the car, say nothing. He keeps up the conversation, wants me to talk, too. "Don't you agree?" he says. He wants me to make it easy on everyone, these good friends who are driving us there. They all keep saying she'll be fine; they'll do all they can. They smile. His face creases. His eyes do not smile. I can hold out no longer, put my head in his lap. They can keep on talking. I sink deep into the question. The choice.

Suddenly it bursts in on me, the obvious, she's been dead all this time. Three hours till they phoned us, three hours for the plane, two more on the road. Her clothes cut away. The snow, the wind, the sirens in unhearing ears. Her hands are open. Each hand dearer than my life. Known to me. Known like that to me alone. I cry no sound.

Hands are on my arms. The priest, his hands shaking, trying to hold me steady as we walk. I'm pressed against him. I say, "It's awful." "I know," he says. "No, you can't know." "I do know," he says, "but we must not lose hope." I want to kill him.

He thinks his arms comfort me. I can't breathe. He tells us to sit in this orange room. Have coffee. Wait for a nurse to come and explain. There is nothing to explain. I will see with my own eyes. I will wait no longer.

I run. The hall is long and dark. A nurse catches up, she is talking. I stop at the door of the glass room, the curtains are drawn. I will pull them aside, it will be someone else's child, mine will walk in and hug me. I pull them aside, she is there in the bed, eyes closed, head turned toward the respirator. I lay my head on her chest.

STANDING BY THE COFFIN, YOU CONSOLE ME

You say some greater good
will come of this death. What good
so great can ever come
from the blood on my house
the stoop of her father's shoulders
the fear in the breath of the children.
She was spared, you say,
the pain of this world. And
its music, savories, skins.
She lives in glory, God's mysterious
twisted ways. Only the good,
you say, die young.

I should have made her wicked,
made her creep out the window
at night, lift money
from my purse, steal my car,
flunk out of school. Then
I could have kept her.
Yelled and grounded her,
followed her to her room and held her, yes,
put my arms around her, held
her howls to my neck,
shook with her

and then, years from now,
could I still keep her?
See her coming in the side door
with a baby on her hip
and a child by the hand
climbing up the steps to me.

FROM ROOM TO ROOM

Each night I touch the foreheads
of my sleeping children.
Deep among the bears and blankets
Julie stirs as I breathe over her,
taking in her warmth.
I tuck her foot under the covers,
leave the night-light on.

Open Tricia's door to dark and silence.
Step over unfinished Monopoly.
Sixth grade—the long, thin body
growing under the comforter.

At Stephanie's door I knock and wait.
Sixteen is not sweet.
Headphones on, floor strewn
with jeans and notebooks.
"'Night, Mom. Close the door." That's all.

Kris's room.
No forehead here to touch.
All her clothes hanging in the closet,
shoes side by side.
The silver crucifix.
A corsage drying by the mirror.

CAN YOU SEE

The sun is shining today.
My feet pound into the snow,
make tracks to your new grave
on this rise where wind
erases any signs
of us, of you.
Can you see me here?

I would have called you Sunday to ask
if calculus was getting easier,
if you'd had a date that wasn't
a dweeb or a drunk.

You wanted to fall in love, real love.
He would talk of stars,
you would dance in the kitchen.
        We'd have fun, Mom, mostly fun.

Backhoe groaning up the hill
stops across the road, turns,
scrapes back a rectangle
to bare brown grass.
The digger's coming next.
I need to hide, see
no more of graves today,
go home and sit
in the hollow of your room.

Superior, the Day the Ice Broke Up

Away, away from stricken faces in whose eyes I see
the loss I cannot bear.

Go north to a place white and still.
I cannot hold another hand.

Trudge far out onto the crusted cove,
the lake locked, all locked.

Look back to frozen cataracts
rusted into rock. Nothing moves.

Sit granite behind cold glass all night,
all black, no stars, no sound.

At dawn, a great crack shakes me.

Out there, where yesterday I walked,
ice boulders roil in blue-black waves.

DID YOU KNOW

when you woke up in your room
that morning

did you feel the brush
of the angel's wing

did it chill you
as you headed for the shower

could you smell in the air
that fragrance

of the last day

THE GROUNDSKEEPERS

Tired old men in loose gray coveralls
heavy boots.
They drive the dirt-filled truck
along green rows, between markers,
then stop, get out.
A melody from the radio
escapes, clipped as the door slams.

They shovel dirt into a new grave
digging it in
turning it over
smoothing
getting ready for sod
for Memorial Day.

Hands wiped on canvas legs
they throw the shovels into the truck
and move along.

Seated in the grass
I am in their way.
Under this brown rectangle of earth
my daughter lies, caged
in oak and velvet, gone to the care
of tired old men
and shovels and sod.

THE WOMAN WHO WAILED

the woman who wailed
    in the grass, in the spring
    wailed on the hill
    on her knees in the spring
the woman who wailed
    with the sound from her knees
    with the sound coming out
    from her belly and knees
the sound ripping out
    spilling life on the ground
    on the blanket of sod
    newly placed on the earth
wailed at the grass
    laid across the bare earth
    fit into the rectangle
    cut in the ground
tore with her fingernails
    into the roots
    of the barrier sod
    between her and her child
crouched on the hill
    with the rushes of sound
    choking on phlegm
    in the wails in the grass
the woman who wailed
    unable to stand
    grinding the daffodils
    under her hand
the woman who wailed
the woman who wailed

DIES IRAE

nightlong the push the sweat the vomit

      exultation
              sleep

9-7-66
that day of birth

K-R-I-S-T-I-N
I signed

for county records
spelling

each letter double-checking
smile of wonder pulling at my face

I held you
ceremonious that moment

swathed in pink crochet, spelled
my own name on the line marked "mother"

and in some county basement now
a new certificate, another date

my fingers trace these grooves
etched in granite in the grass

Your First Birthday after Death

"Sing up to the sky,"
the youngest insisted.
"On somebody's birthday, you sing."

"A cake, mint frosting."
The next child carried it, wobbling,
outside, down the back steps.

The third one left. "Bizarre," she said.

Gold from evening clouds
pushed through the maple's shadow.
Your father flared a match,
nineteen candles.
Still air pulled the flames straight.

Our ragged voices slid together
      birthday
           happy
                to you

One balloon floated.
Sisters blew across the cake.

IMPERATIVE

It's the thing they can't imagine,
the sacrifice no one dares
to contemplate

nor can they look you in the eye
when, if you should dare,
you speak its name.

You are beseeched
to wave it off, apologize
for conduct unbecoming.

Duck your head,
change the subject,
promise with a smile

that they need never understand,
that the words for this are foreign
and defy translation.

You Come Back

to a house by a creek
under damp green shadows
you look pale
your smile is tired
you need iron and more sleep
they don't feed you over there

we stand around the kitchen
your friends sitting on the counters
rock music strangely out of place
we are hushed behind our smiles
breathe in short gasps

you put your arms around me
say, *Mother, let me go*

bones hold me, flesh is thin
I feel in your shoulders
the other
you are other

Proceedings

Pursuant to you killed my daughter
this legal document
plaintiffs on the icy road in Indiana
how you slid defendant Gordon Carey
across the median into their lane
U.S. 31 and 16th Street a Friday afternoon
injuries sustained Federal Court in
Minnesota attorney number 52906
summons and complaint sirens snowing
pinned in the front seat of a red VW
now see this summons and complaint
on ivory paper toll the statute of
limitations our pecuniary loss
the cotrustees for the heirs of our
dead Kristin
in the snow by the side of the highway
glass and snowflakes sparkle in the white air
IV arrest heart-needle adrenalin
the CAT scan the
darkness cerebral hemorrhage
failed to keep safe lookout
bleeding into the ventricles
I wiped the blood from her ear
failed to operate the vehicle
on the right side of the road the call the
Marshall County Sheriff's Office we
flew to Chicago missed the last
plane drove two hours to South Bend the
chaplain said wait in this orange room while

I get a nurse no not one minute longer
I'm going to see her now but
pursuant to the laws of the state of
Minnesota in the dark corridors with
night-lights my boots running to the
glassed-in room pull back the striped curtains
monitor blinking red respirator oh God
respirator makes you breathe against your
will don't die don't die therefore
summons therefore summons and
complaint you killed her
in the blinding snow

HER GRAVE IS ON A HILL

The salesman drove us slowly
up the glazed incline
held my elbow as he trudged us up the hill
my cold feet lifting, plunging
through the drifts. No monument protruded
from the snow, the only landmark
an acute angle of bare anonymous bushes
clicking in the wind

nothing here but charts
whipping on the clipboard in his hand
and his words
dashed into my ears

> *desirable feature*
> *you'll like this spot*

*

Her grave is on a hill.
Young crabapples drip with flowers
that bud deep rose
and pale by moments as they open.
It's a short life. Going gray,
the petals fall to the ground,
are rained into pulp.
Blades of grass bend over them,
hold them in the wispy air
until the mower comes.

The bushes green up in spring,
go brown and brittle in the fall.
Even underneath them, every inch of ground
is marked for graves, each no larger
than a coffin's width and length.
The plat is displayed under glass
on the counter in the office.
When demand grows, the backhoe
will uproot the shrubs
to open up another section.
Down the hill a bank of lilacs
disappeared this week.

SURVIVOR

I will live a very long time.
I will see all I love taken from me.
This walk of grief I will repeat,
more years like this very long year.

I will answer another telephone
freeze my blood rush to listen more closely
to hear an official voice tell me
There's been an accident, ma'am.

I will fly again through midnight
to a city I never thought of,
the clock's red digital minutes
between the living and me.

I will sit at a hospital bedside
croon lullabies into the closed ear
press hands on the arm of my dear one
pump warmth from my skin to the cold one.

I will live a very long time
past every person I love.
My closet is ready with charcoal and navy.
My step will grow measured and slow.

I will slide to my place in the pew
ride cushioned in black limousines.
I will walk to the graveyard, familiar,
kneel in the grass of my life work.

I will sit on the ash heap of mourning
surrounded by clothing and pictures
accept all the visits and flowers
rock by the hearth growing smaller.

I wanted to die my own death,
to bleed, to put brakes on my breathing.
but I am too tough to extinguish.
My dead child has taught me survival.
I will live a very long time.

ALDEBARAN

The child does not wait for me
though I climb past orange groves

through pines, to the grassy plain
of Palomar. The scleral dome sees

a new galaxy flaming into birth
on the edge of the universe.

I circle the building, hands in my pockets,
shoulders hunching toward new stars.

Strung above me, layers of stars
spiral toward heaven. I grasp

the struts of the universe, hoist
myself through the black gridwork

where each star hangs, around Polaris,
hinge of the constellations,

to Cygnus, the swan, the sisters Pleiades,
and the follower, Aldebaran.

Then I am back on the mountain, where
cold inspired air seeps thinly

through lungs into muscle, into bone.
The silent astronomers turn

their faces to the giant lens.
Look, I tell them, over the edge for me.

Find the new star born
the day she died.

Look now, over the edge to God
and the lost members of ourselves.

IF YOU WALK WITH ME

Blown, when she died,
to hot fragments in the sky
I hung, a cloud of ash in the air,
changing the color of sunlight.

Cooling, settling to cinders
on the black lava slope
I watch for forsythia.
I know that it will pierce the crust

and I will stand, hold my face
to its yellow branch
and walk the circle
of the mountain.

Beneath my feet
the volcano rumbles.
Be careful if you walk with me.

Now

Her long hair, thick but weightless
lifts in the breeze like innocent flames
or streams out behind her like Atalanta's.
She will need the strength of Atalanta to prevail.

As she rides hard along the road,
she is not alone. A specter
rides beside her, keeping pace
when she surges or falls back.
The specter is neither past nor future
but the present, incomplete, as it will always be.

The longer they ride together,
the more familiar the ride becomes,
until she cannot remember
when she rode alone.

II. God's Hands

GOD'S HANDS LOOK SO BUSY FROM HERE

after Deborah Keenan

Put your trouble in the hands of God,
you say, he'll provide, he'll shelter,
he'll clothe in glory glory
but God's hands look busy and so full
that sometimes he must drop things
over the sides and between those
fingers ringed by the daily prayers
of the creatures of this planet.
Do the elephants pray and do click-beetles,
does the hummingbird pray for nectar
or aerodynamics? No wonder
the hands of God are busy,
cupped as they are around
Earth's supplications.

And what
of the other planets, here,
and in Andromeda and all
those spiral galaxies whose creatures
we do not know, cannot recognize,
would not count as life because
they are not like us,
their eyes not like our eyes,
their senses, perhaps, not even
like our senses, so that
we could not sing to them
or feed them, would not
accord them notice,

being fixed in our universe
where God is in our image and
his hands like our hands fumble
at holding on and letting go.

THE YEAR THE CHERRIES WERE SO GOOD

In a circle of heaped fruit
Mother sat on the side porch
her legs dangling over the edge.
Her hands sorted cherries
from the pool in her apron—
for pies, for canning, for jelly.

Dad, humming high in the cherry tree,
lowered the full pail on its rope,
hand over hand to me.
"This one is yours, Liz."
I slid my fingers through the depth of cherries,
rolled the crimson pebbles over my palms.
All that I could hold, I ate,
jarring my teeth on hard centers,
rubbing my cheeks with dark juice.

Mother sat silent. Her eyes
flicked upward at him
but could not hold in that direction,
saw only the air
between his sneakers and
the hard unloving ground,
felt only the moments it could take
his strong young body
to slice from branch to ground.

Toward the little boys, hanging
by their knees from lower branches,
she hissed

hold on tight
don't touch the rope

"Relax, honey," he called to her.
He didn't fall.
Not my Dad.

After that year the bloom diminished,
the cherries were fewer,
birds ate most of them.
Tall enough, we picked from stepladders.
Then the old tree was gone.

I never saw the pail
ride the rope to the top again,
nor my father, arms upreaching,
sway toward the sky.

WITHOUT PERIL

She was higher above the earth
than she had ever been. The air

was sharper in her nose
than it had ever been,

tinged with the sharp smell of pitch
sticky in her palms. She had never

climbed a tree before. He had dared her,
the boy whose smile glinted in the dappled light.

The tree, kind to an ingénue,
arranged its limbs like steps.

She could reach each one above the next
without peril.

As she climbed, the soft needles
brushed her cheeks, her hair.

Mother would know where she had been
by their fragrance. At the top

she parted the branches and looked out
over the fields. A white bird rising.

IN THE SHADOW OF MY HOUSE

Outside your door I'd call you
Jeeee-niee.
We'd spread a blanket on the hill
in the pointed shadow of my house
and play dress-up. You
were always Marge. I was Eileen.
In old gowns, Mother's lipstick
worn to the sharp rim,
we'd dance to the radio—
"Shrimp Boats Are A-Coming"—
waving a rosy scarf to the horizon,
the field beyond the apple tree.

At night we played Witches and Fairies.
I the Queen, of course, climbed
the iron railing on the front steps
to taunt our brothers, the witches.
They chased us into the dark
rhubarb behind the garage,
lay across us in the damp grass.
> *how the white clapboards caught the kitchen light*
> *how the night air condensed around us*

We played at my house mostly.
Your father, his darkness
in midafternoon. He parked
his car in the grass.

The last time we met
I washed your mother

after her breasts were removed.
You came into that cold room
blanched, holding flowers.
We could not speak.

I left our town, but Mother sends news
of babies, business. Your divorce.
Today I read your brother died of AIDS.

I remember the summer we strung a basket
between our bedroom windows
  meet me in the pine trees
it bumped on the roof of the new addition,
the handle caught on the gable
and sometimes stuck.
  meet me in the pine trees

ALWAYS

The face on the old sheet music
is a face like her mother's,
if she can imagine her mother
so young and so dreamy,

her head leaning back,
dark hair waving over her shoulders,
teeth gleaming in her half-open mouth,
eyes looking out in rapture.

She thinks of the face as her mother's,
that shy, practical woman,
whom she has never seen
transported past duty.

She remembers a snapshot, its edges
crumbled from years in her father's wallet:
The slight figure clasps a purse in both hands.
The shoulders hunch in the summer dress

pulling the waistband up a fraction,
lifting the hem just above the knees.
The young woman, not yet her mother,
smiles, white teeth parting her lips.

The man who loves her snaps the shutter,
and she runs forward to catch his arm.
Her wide eyes absorb his slender height,
the just-pressed uniform, the bars on his collar.

He will leave soon, the picture in his wallet,
but she does not think about that.
She hears, he hears, the music of the song
he whistles still—"Always."

SOMETHING NEW

In pinafore and buckle shoes
she stands
just outside the door
watching
as quiet as she can be.

Through bedroom shadows
white skin shines.
Her mother wears no shirt,
sits rigid in the bed,
her legs out straight beneath the spread.

The two breasts gleam
against black waves of hair,
one dark nipple.

The other, the other
is in the baby's mouth.
The woman's eyes flick
toward the door.

Go play
she says.

STRAWBERRIES

dirt beneath
my fingernails

fruit hairy
in my mouth

then crushed, simmering
by the red Formica table

on which rest all
our memories

and a mother
who is always there

in an apron or out but
always there

in her skin like a peach
as she tells me about signs

in Springfield store windows
No Irish Need Apply

though the windows hung with lace
the ceilings hung with song

that fragrance
hanging

in the pluvial air
of a red kitchen

my fingers sweet
with jelly juice

GOING OVER THE BRIDGE

Daddy whistles in the front seat.
Mother's lips are set
in the half-smile she wears
when she dresses us up
and takes us out.
It's the old Chevy, but—

> the back door is open
> I can feel air moving
> smell the river approaching
> it is happening again—

> the bridge has no railings
> car has no wheels, just
> sleigh runners, red ones,
> curled around in the front,
> pointed straight in the back,
> and sliding, sliding over the edge—

Daddy turns to me, grins, as I
lean into the open door.
Don't worry, Ace.
the car tilts toward water.
Your Dad
won't let anything
happen to you.

HOMESTEAD AVENUE

after Robert Francis

firefly	backporch	swingset
kickball	nightgame	streetlamp
schoolbus	haircut	clownface
halloween	dutchgirl	bearpit
snowflake	hillside	bootbuckle
tensiontower	pinetree	birchbark
crabapple	boyfriend	frontporch
willowtree	driveway	lighthouse
sandflea	Cape Cod	dunegrass
seaspray	bowsprit	summer

First Kiss

He's practiced at this,
I can tell. I am not,
though I am eager because
soon I'll be sixteen and
nothing in the third-grade coatroom
can rightly be called a kiss
despite revisionist dreams.

Wet. His big lips.
Mine soft but not too open
so there are teeth bumping.
The white sofa under me
in my girlfriend's living room
as her cousin turns to me,
comes closer, smiles.

Past his shoulder the sofa
is still white. My lips, however,
are no longer virgin.

WE COME HOME

There was the hollowness of the apartment
as I stood alone, watching the silent newborn.

There was my fear as she stretched in the seat,
beginning to wake, to want, to need.

I held my breath as her eyes opened,
lids peeling apart from each other,

saw the fragility of her milky skin
suffused with her own incandescence.

There was the independent pumping of her heart
and my hand daringly placed on her chest,

the delicate throb of her body,
that small sigh, not sorrow, not pain,

but awareness of earth.
There was the stab in my groin

as a gaze held between us,
pull of my arms toward her squirm,

lift of my palms under the heavy head
and the weightless spine.

There was her flesh fragrant in my face,
her breath against my neck.

His Mother Talks at Dinner

I don't need a chair. I'll just stand here by the stove. It's real handy. We always had to serve The Men. We had to cook for The Men, ya, a big forenoon lunch every day. You finish it. I'm not hungry. I'll just eat this neck here. Cut that last piece up in three. You each take one. All I got is store-bought cookies for dessert.

The bugger. If I got hold of him, I'd cut them things right off. He got no right to do that to a girl. Baby's crying. She's not satisfied. You sure you got enough milk? Maybe she needs a bottle. Let Grandma help. We don't want her going hungry. Poor little thing. Come to Grandma. He's a kind man, my son is. One thing you got to say about him is he's kind. Oh, we had so much beef on the farm. I don't even like the look of steak. Is she warm enough? You got an undershirt on her? Maybe her feet are cold. We got to count our blessings. You got your health, you got everything. It could be worse.

What a Child Must Carry

Compressible to eight inches
Jessica toddled through
the sunny yard
stumbled on the
flowerpot
and dropped
through the iron pipe.

In Midland, Texas, in October 1987,
diamond bits are breaking on adamant
twenty-nine feet underground.
Chippers and drillers jackhammer
in thirty-minute shifts,
come up to sob and vomit
in the trampled grass.
Her mother, face hanging in the tube,
wails of ducklings and
a fortitude she does not know
as the child consorts with Charon.
For fifty-eight hours
media words reach into kitchens

as the first paramedic,
coming up from underneath,
lubricates the pipe,
tugs down against her whimpers,

and hands her to the second,
who holds her to his chest
for the ride up

to the bawling men
and the women singing
by the ambulance,
to camera glare

and who will get
the movie rights,
to surgical opinions
and the tribute
of one small dead toe,
darkness, ice cream
and all that a child must carry.

TWELVE-AND-A-HALF

Can I peel the potatoes for you? she asks
and *I like your nail polish, Mom.*

She tells me what Sarah said
and what Jennifer said
and *what I said, Mom.*
Her eyes redden over the sink
as we bake together. I rub my floury hand
between her shoulder blades,
press love along her knobby spine, now

in this moment, before
the yeast rises, now
in this moment, when
she will allow me
to be kind.

FLIGHT FROM DETROIT
Northwest Flight 255, August 16, 1987

Did they know at seven seconds
and how long
did they hang in fear
and at nineteen seconds
did they know that flaps and slats
were not extended
that not enough vacuum could be produced
above the slender wings
to pull the plane into
that abhorring space
over Detroit
where now I see the yellow vinyl bags
strewn through engine parts and
scorched aluminum skin

like the skin of the little girl
pried from her mother's two thin arms,
arms swelled to cushion her
without airbag, without foam
against the tarmac skid
just mother's arms doing what they do
as she turned her white blouse to the flames
to shield the child Cecilia

who carries with her now
the empty sound of the checklist
the taste of asbestos and ash
the smell of last seconds ticking
all of her life.

Three Teeth in a Brown Envelope

They shut me out as you go under,
put me in the waiting room.
You count backward from a hundred.
Walls float.
Who is with you, child, as I sit
outside the door, a magazine in my lap
describing travel to the Outer Islands?

From somewhere a voice—
        "You may come in now."

Packs in your oozing mouth,
you cry anesthesia tears.
Half-sitting against the pillowed wall,
you swivel, lean your long adolescent
spine into my shoulder,
accept my arm around you,
my cheek on your soft hair.

UNDER THIS BROKEN SKY

A loon call trembles.
Water ripples on the shore,
a sound of ease and good life.
High clouds scud across the sun
as I think of your son
a boy in my kitchen
as I think of your son and his gun—

> was it sunny in the field that day
> and how long did he lie there alone
> till they called you
> back from the mountains
> how did they know—
> how did they know he was yours—

Now that we know of your son, and his gun,
there's the telephone,
and packing to get back to town.
My daughters cover the boat.
They understand about death,
put away skis, the rake, the float
as I lie flat
under this broken sky.

Swallows swoop over me
collecting mosquitoes.
A heron dives to the water,
spears a fish, and rises to a tree.
Somewhere you are driving toward
home and your terrible task.
There is thunder in the clouds.

Halley Watch, 1986

for Jeanne

Alone on the Easter beach at 4:00 a.m.
away from the lights of San Diego Bay—
     of aircraft carriers, four of them,
     across from a steamboat dining palace—

I track the stars along the dark horizon.
The comet should be west of Scorpio's tail,
streaking through the night as it did
in 1910, when it swiped the earth with brilliance.

All winter I have scanned the sky in vain—
     from a roof at Christmas in St. Paul
     where an astronomer gestured through the cold
     to a pinpoint coming toward us from deep space—

     from a cold Lenten pasture in New England
     where morning twilight, sucked into cirrus threads
     above the trees, veiled the sparkling dust and gas
     blown to feathers in the solar wind.

My feet in the cold sand, I walk the shore,
get behind a cliff to shadow out
the wan vapor lamps of parking lots.

Black sea, white waves.
Black sky, white stars.

Three times I pass a gray smudge near Centaurus.
Three times I wipe the lens of the binoculars

then recognize
the rising fuzz ball in the sky
not bright, not glorious, simply

a dandelion's pulsing head
faint seeds spurring from the center.

Foam around my ankles
I rush toward sea and night
breathe in, hold, and blow

over water, into heaven
scattering celestial seeds.

To Pablo Neruda, from His Mother, with Love

Remember when I held you last,
when I blessed you
in your natal name, Neftali,
when my eyes pressed into yours
the lives of all the families before you.
Think of that now, you who are called
The Poet
by those who endure
down the long spine
of our *slim nation.*
I speak to you of "*Pasado.*"
I am uneasy to see this poem, my son.

*

You say, *We have to discard the past.*
You know it cannot be done.
The past sings in each tree
that has sprung from a seed.
Your poems, so brave, so beautiful,
have returned to our people the force
of the Chilean past *before wig and frockcoat.*

First broken tiles,
then *pompous doors,*
the past can be judged but never destroyed.
The present cannot be *an empty plate.*

How can you say
There is nothing; there is always nothing?
Think, Pablo, think of the rich beauty

of your Sweet Country, how
the foam of the world rises from its seaboard
how *the violets are at home in the earth.*

Is this nothing?
I do not admit such nothing.

When *downward*
tumbles yesterday
as in a well
falls yesterday's water
it mingles with the floods of other yesterdays
not gone but waiting, waiting
to be drunk again. You think you can
teach bones
to disappear
but bones, water
wait unseen in the earth.

*

Remember the scarlet fish, Neftali,
how you ran to our hut crying
of its beauty and cast for days
into the water to catch it? The fish
burned its scarlet on your eye
that day in Temuco.

Do not say to your mother
it has been; it has been and now
memories mean nothing.
Say to me: "I have to remember everything."

You have accepted the obligation of the poet:
I am here to tell the story,
and I honor you,
as a mother to her son,
as a Chilean woman to her Poet.

*

Dear Poet, dear son,
dear Comrade Pablo Neruda,
I write to you for your strength.
They call you Senator, Ambassador.
In the cities and in the *cordilleras*
they repeat your verse.
You will wear the laurel,
your dreams will have their glory
and your friend Allende his reforms.
You will feel *the giant anaconda . . .*
like the circle of the earth
rising through the threat and the salvation.

Do not see the river
flowing through your house.
Do not see the borrowed grave
where you will lie.
When they drive your *compañeros*
into Chile Stadium, do not believe
that what once was, was and is lost,
lost in the past, and now will not return.

One woman will whisper,
"Here, with us, now and forever,"
and they will remember
everything.

DAUGHTER OF KINETIC AIR

In the calm
I think of you,
the child
whose passage
through the room
sparks

against me.
The same fire
links and kindles us.
Dust devils
skitter
out of our way.

Full of angst,
you yearn to go,
though not yet ready
to be safe alone.
Still, you are more
woman than child,

pathfinder in the journey
only you can make.

Geography Lesson

My nephew has left for Turkey, or is it Saudi, he can't say
but he called his father, my brother,
who called our mother
who called me
to say, *The boy has gone to Saudi or is it Turkey,*
to defend a line in the sand that isn't on the map
I studied in color-coded shapes in fourth grade
when I first learned of Geography:

> *Welcome to Pedro's world,* a land called Argentina,
> *Welcome to Chin Lee's world,* so far outside my yard,

their shaded faces upturned on the page, smiling
from other hemispheres.

A new word, *hemisphere,* like *latitude, plateau,*
and *products,* drawn in tiny shapes inside each country's
boundaries—forest products, minerals, sheep, and oil, latticed
derricks marching on the map like any natural resource, like tin
or agriculture, derricks hardly distinguishable in shape and size
from sheaves of wheat.

I did not see the money changing hands as the teacher
talked of trade.

I did see the marketplace, the tented stalls, the smiles of
bargainers who cart their *produce*—another new word—
who cart their carrots, rutabagas, grapefruit to the plaza
for my fluffy wool, my homespun, my tightly woven tapestries.

I did not hear the clink of coins in the pot, slip of dollars into
pockets and the sigh of power from the lungs of those who hold
their produce to their chests and circumscribe their carts in the
bazaar with lines dragged by sticks in that oily desert sand.

Palestine I heard of, Lebanon, the land of Israel emerging in the
teacher's talk but not yet printed in our old texts. No one told us
of the conflict over territory, there was no Middle East,
just a Holy Land with camels and hooded figures
silhouetted in the desert night, bearing gifts.
I knew nothing of Arabia, there was no

smiling Yussef on page eight to say
        Welcome to my world,
nothing of Koran or Torah, *oasis* or *mirage*
and now our boy aboard a cargo plane flies from Kansas with
The First Army of the United States—*Patton's army, The Big Red One*
he says with pride—

to another land of flat expanse, a hurried call to home before liftoff,
a postcard to Vermont stamped and ready to slide into a mail bag:
        It's quiet here, thanks for everything at Christmas,
        the weather's fine, which means:
        I've gone to war and they won't let me call you—
a card that Grandma, who remembers war,
slipped into his pocket, whispering—
        If you can't call us, drop this in the mail
        so we'll know when you've gone

to Geography. But he did call,
We're shipping out, the tanks already are on railroad cars, we are
climbing into C-5As,
I'm ready, I'll kick butt, we'll show them

which is how you must go into war if you're the boy behind the
gun, my brother's boy, smiling as he held up to the camera
his six-layer torte ringed with berries—
     I'll go to hotel school when I come back—
smiling over strawberries that shine through a glaze
like the frost melting on my window
as we start another lesson in

Geography, the one on power,
with no new friend smiling from the page
to welcome us with products of his native land.

STEPHANIE'S WOLVES

I will not scream or
jump into the front seat.

Not for you, dogs, will I stand this ground
but for her, my daughter,

who asks me to sleep
on her floor tonight—with you—

and, dammit, I will, and
you may eat me or

not eat me there is
nothing I will not

do for her can you
love her that much

you strange creatures
part dog, part wolf

that Stephanie rocks
as if you were her babies.

She and I have battled each other
and now we don't and I will prove it.

I love her this much: Tonight
I will lie down with you.

She Invites Me to the Mountains

I lie on a mattress on the floor of her room,
watch rocks go red high overhead, balanced
against each other long enough
to grow moss and mountain grasses.
Something is working here
among the boulders.
Small flowers curl up from the base of rocks,
lay themselves over hard edges,
turning to the sun.

The sky, which yesterday was overcast,
is clear mountain blue, as she promised.
My breath comes easy now as I rest
in my daughter's house. My heart, which pounded
as I followed her through thin air among the crags,
slows to steady, still enough in this high meadow
to let past labors go in the evening song of birds.
My voice returns. I do not have to talk,
find something delicate to say.

What My Father Said

if you laugh, *if you don't weaken*
toward despair, life is sweet

it's a great life, he said,
if you don't weaken, then

he winked at me and chuckled
so I knew it was important

and say it now to my children
my commandment, too

as true as the ones on stone
it's a great life if you don't weaken

though I can't wink
can only catch my breath

for wanting them to believe
that it's a sweet life in the morning

in spite of all the anguish
not because your strength is rigid

not because there's just one way
but because you bend toward happiness

like shining copper wire
and flex like a muscle that is doing its work

true strength is tensile, *relax,* he said
it's a great life if you don't weaken

PAST PICTURES

for Mary Anne

The summer night settles damp across my lap
as we remember raising children here together.
No longer do we meet at the swimming pool.
Your daughter's in New Zealand now, mine's in France.

In the thick dark
        beneath your maple tree
                a light sparks—

we flash to the kitchen—
        sweep the shelves for a jelly jar—
                grab an ice pick, jab the lid—

and leap, grown women
        through the black yard
                scooping bugs into glass.

In my hands past pictures click from insect bellies—
little girls, hair flowing in the moonlight,
run fearless through the dark,
then flicker out.

PRAYER FOR CHILDREN

after Mary Oliver

You do not have to be safe.
You do not have to stay in your room
locked against disaster.

It may never find you in the wild,
yet may trace you to your tower.
Believe:
I know this.

Slip out the back window
      run up the hill, twirl yourself
            starward. Let your arms knife the dark.
                Let despair fly out from the center
                    through your fingertips.

When I chase you,
    step behind glass.
          When I scream, wave.
             Swim bravely downriver
                to the open ocean!

In its own time
your heart,
which was born
beating
in this circle,
will find its way
home.

III. SOMETHING

WHAT HOLDS

Not love.
Not that look of trust
in the back seat of the wedding car.
Not power, which is pressed
into the marriage, claimed
in the placing of spoon and knife
on table.
Nor yielding.
In the giving up to air
of all one's choice
is still no peace.
What holds is plodding. One foot,
one day. As the tumor casts
one cell upon another,
as the child one slow tooth.
The story one word.
No return.
No living out again
with new regard. This—
treading through the year.

Loons for Life

Are they happy
or do they work from duty?
He lifts his gleaming breast
above the water, as she
slides chicks into the reeds
while my head is turned.

He beats his wings and calls.
Is it song or instinct
or exercise of lung and throat?
Is it sunset, summer, or
a query and an answer:

> *Are you there?*
> *I am here*
> *and it will soon be night:*
> *Come home.*

In fall they leave the cooling water
but return in spring to breed,
to incubate, instruct, and nurture chicks

and call to one another
evenings,
from bay to bay
across the open water.

Two Chairs and an Umbrella Table

We are protected here.
The mountains surround us.
Wind from the hills
blows away all terrors, and
smoke rises into dreams.
Come to the table,
sit on the bull's-eye.

Two chairs for two people:
Where have you gone?
Come back to this table,
lean in, pull the chairs closer.
This is the place
of contentment.

Hunger

At Rice, Minnesota,
where the road curves sharply north

and a white steepled church
thrusts forward past stone graves

I lean into the turn
let go the wheel of the car

and slide toward the side
near a bright green sign

Rice, A Star City
Population 289

each life as precious as mine
each life with pain and yet

those lives make love in the night
when pain can be forgiven

when compassion can ignite
in skin against skin

in the dark hunger
where light can spark

across the separate troughs
pressed into our bed

and years of sleep
on no common ground.

THE EDGE OF LONELINESS

dumped
washed
set before me
empty
not even bitters

this taste
of nothing
is new

McCarey

5513 Brokview Ave
Edina, Mn
          55436

No Language for This

I fold half the towels from our bathroom,
stack them in a laundry basket, add the blue ones
for when the children will visit him.
Which pots and pans? I ask.
Blank-eyed, he says, *For cooking?*

Which sheets for your new bed?
Don't tell me about that bed,
not its size
or who will sleep there.
No language for this,
for the end of the story . . .

The children sit in the den.
We say the word *separate.*
One cries.
The youngest, bewildered, looks at me.
The oldest, who remembers heat, says
"A good idea, any marriage needs . . ."

needs something we do not have
cannot find
won't look for
beyond the wasteland bed
where he sprawled,
I still hang on the edge.

After You Left, I

slept until 10:30, one eye
peering through dreams to the sunlit sky
its untroubled turquoise striped
by black balsam branches
battered in the northwest wind

made coffee, warmed a muffin,
drank juice by the glass wall
the ice thinning to black
where the lake moves beneath
before the ice breaks

THE STRING OF BETRAYAL PLUCKED

its strange notes in a twelve-tone mode
neither dissonance nor melody
insistent, though I tried not to listen. Later,
when I could no longer practice deafness,
when notes resounded all around me,
I began to hear the tune and it was
ugly. The only way to shut it out
was to sing against it. Though I was tired
and the wind was blowing, I kept on.
In the cacophony I heard the one true tone.
I followed it out the door and,
picking up a lute, began to strum.
An echo from the cliff wall
guided me.

SOMETHING

were we something
or was it all just dribbled away
like unfulfilled coition

were we something
do the children know
did we give them something

will they say
>*weren't they something*
>*before they fell from grace*

will they remember
perhaps the garden
how it grew

how each flopping flower,
nudged upright,
had a twig to lean on

or perhaps the laden table
the men stretched out
after feasting

the porch swing in twilight
or the hum above our heads
of something bright

What He Said When I Asked Why

> *sufficiently*
a reasonable request
sufficiently was all he asked
> *you were not sufficiently*

who among us is sufficient
unto the day, the task, desire
reliable at the stove, perhaps, thriving
on bread and coffee, present
by the stairs with guiding hand, steadfast
by the side of the big man, shaking
hands, dimpling, becoming
with my biggest eyes the best
Nancy Reagan I could manage
considering [*you were not sufficiently*]
what was that again   *not sufficiently*
> *adoring*

EVERYTHING IS EXPERIMENT

getting into a Dodge Polara with a pink lampshade
in the rear window angled to allow the driver
to look through it unimpeded except for the ruffled edge
but that was small and dainty, getting into a black Dodge
and setting off across the continent for the first time
a continent mapped with rivers, red highways, and blue
its capital cities with stars, its villages, towns—
setting off, nevertheless, into the wild
in the arms of a love young and singing

everything is experiment: in bed with a man, his long body
his hands and the blaze thereafter, the bodies together
igniting life after life and then the experiment ultimate
new lives
                         What do I do now?
The first needs are easy though constant and no mistaking them
no confusing who's responsible, who's on duty night and day
intake, output, safety, the whole experiment laid out
by nature between bodies and the universe closes in
to a sharp focus, the door closes on a second floor apartment
and I rise to the experiment.

Cheer up, my mother chuckles, it gets worse—
when walking starts, and talking, and behind the wheel it does,
everything is experiment after that, though with more certainty,
some wisdom and I learn from each experiment but still, when doors
slam in the midst of celebrations the next move is experiment
how to hold the focus, keep the door ajar or lock it
when occasion warrants.

                    Occasion warranted.
I locked a door, the universe closed again to a sharp focus
everything after that has been experiment, beginning
like all experiments in hypothesis, followed by testing
and the search for proofs, the elation of success, the pit
of failure, doors open, they close, the work is never finished
everything is experiment.

A WOMAN SITTING ON A ROCK

If she wants to fish, she must
cast her own line,
she must bait it herself,
she must not wait, dimpling,
for someone else to lay
his hand on her, his hand slick
with fish guts and squid.

She must lift the pole
over her head, snap
with her own wrist, watch
with her own eyes
how the fly dances
how the line lies on the water

not ask, where did it go
where did it all go
when she was not looking
when she was looking around.
She must watch for herself

and let a kind man
appear or not appear,
let him tend his own line, let them
catch or not catch, let them
eat their catch together or alone

but let her not be waiting in hope or in vain
on these rocks of basalt, feldspar, quartz,
let her not be lost, gazing out past the tide

to that line of rest beyond the shoals,
out where the color deepens.

PART TWO

IV. ENOUGH

No Ordinary Tree

You know this is not an ordinary
tree, no one has hung from it, understand,
though its thick limbs rise at just the right angle,
just the right height from the ground
to serve

the purpose
or some other purpose, shelter, perhaps
for a flock of doves or ravens
in the middle of the vast expanse of prairie
or a traveler's mark on the horizon
with miles and days to go as the tree appears, recedes

in wind and snow, it stands and bends
lightning doesn't seek it
water rises to its roots
roots as deep as the tree is tall

and in the summer's heat
a green shadow on the golden fields.

GO INTO THE DESERT

The desert is beautiful and it is not empty.
Sand shifts along an unseen plate
and each new pattern
signals to the waiting eye—

this, or not that
here, and then there—
while the eye follows undulations
of an inner sea, crest and trough

of each wave. Life is like that—
the ululations of time's throat
fall and rise inside the ear
as sand muffles or reveals

a space in the emptiness
which is not desert,
the desert time
which is not barren.

ENOUGH

How can one tall pine
stand against such wind,
its roots find anchor enough
to hold it on this rocky cliff
against incessant storms

not just last night's thunders
that downed great trees behind me
but against the pounding blizzards
of this far north shore? How?

Species survive because
individuals survive,
snaking down one dainty root—
despite a sparse supply of soil—

into a toehold in the rock,
then pushing deeper
toward stability.

By my feet a chip of rock
has broken away,
and left a pocket
to catch the rain.

Here an errant seed can sprout
and its root, too, snake down,
find perhaps a grain of earth blown in,
enough to live on for a while. Little,
but enough.

THE WOMEN

They bake in hot tiny kitchens,
tie back their Sears Roebuck curtains
to peer out of small trailer windows
into a forest of jack pine.
They, too, are survivors,

rising from fires
that kill weaker species around them.
They keep care of men who drink their defeats,
who chainsaw their small plots of ground,

corner to corner,
carving small dominance
out of trees, into land,
grinning through black-toothed mouths.

*

The women rub Tide into shirts slashed with grease,
hang wash on a line between birches,
sweep cinder block steps
clean of pine needles, webs,
shake the rugs for the doorways.

The women bring bread and a hot dish,
then sit beside the bereaved,
slip ironed hankies from sleeves.

Together they kneel in the quiet church,
amid the exotic flowers.

Each lowers her head
in thanks to her God

for the children who live
the man in her bed
her broom, her soap
her spoons, her thread.

THE FIGURE OF HISTORY

By the slope of the shirt
I know this is a woman.
By the flat of her bare feet
I recognize the labor of her days.
From her hands hang twisted iron bands.
Wordless, she holds them
and stares into eyes
of the one who has thrust
these fragments on her
again.

In another life
she sits under oak,
blue taffeta fanned around her.
She folds her hands in her lap
so as not to wrinkle the silk.
Her feet in white satin rest precisely
side by side on the grass.
Her jaunty partner leans his braided cuff
on the iron settee, points the musket barrel
toward the earth, the hound sniffing.

Once, the woman was an angel
white-clad, light of passage,
her hair gilt in the starlight.
She thought she could heal all.
But the arrows of small boys

brought her down.
Though they bandaged her, and

raised her on a pallet,
her weight bending their steps,

she was broken.
The knowledge of good and evil
could not be repaired,
not by her
not by little boys

whose fathers have schooled them
in the rites of power
whose mothers have laid their delicate palms
across the prickled scalps,
pulling toward the breasts
that define the slope of dress,

the darling boys who suckled once and
must not drink there any more
must be pushed out
which mothers do not want to do

and now these boys
go about the world
searching, searching
for a place to lie
and drink.

SEA GULL

Finally it gives up and sits down
on the stippled rock,
settles itself into its feathers,
turns its head shoreward to me,
the one who will not go away.

No more shrieking or beating of wings
in a mockery of threat. I'm here,
Gull, and I'm staying.
I am bigger than you,
though I know what you do not—

that you could peck my eyes out,
that in a contest you would win.
Until then, I stare you down,
watch you lift one webbed foot
and stretch, as if for battle,

then set it down and lift the other.
Armed and ready, you bury your yellow beak
in the feathers of your breast,
preen out an insect. A tuft of down
sticks to your beak. You look unkempt.

Lobster buoys bob along a line
out from shore where the sea shelf drops.
No matter the waves or the tide,
they hold their place, anchored

to something solid.
The gull approaches, its rubber feet
silent on the rock. It watches me,
turns its head out to sea and back,
watches me again with its yolk-yellow eye

moves a little farther out
and then we settle down,
the gull and I,
each on our ledge

in the seaspray,
in the sunlight
in the silence
when the contest is over.

Shakespeare's Daughters

You know who they are,
the lovely young women
of tragedy, comedy, romance—
Celia, Viola, Hero, and Beatrice
Helena, Hermia, Portia, and Jessica

daughters of fathers who marry them off
to advance the estate,
or fail to and fume
over bad luck or impotence

angry as cuckolds
if the girls don't obey
and what can be worse
than a cuckold.

Miranda, Ophelia,
and poor Desdemona—
Where are their mothers?
Surely these girls—
for that's what they are—

cannot all be Athenas
sprung from paternity,
pompous Polonius, irascible Lear.
Surely there must have been
somewhere a womb.

Whom did they have to tell them
of money and menses and men,

of marriage and then being brought to bed
to live or die in childbirth?

Ah, perhaps I should have said
the mothers all died in childbirth
or the writer was a man
or the product of his age

or they had to use young boys
to play the father's daughters
and older women were too
complicated

ah, yes, complicated. There it is.
A woman wise with years
would never stand for
exile on an island with spirits

but it's more than that.
It's property, it's territory,
ownership that would be
challenged by that other parent
(excepting Lady Capulet).

It's wisdom whispered
in a daughter's ear
that might have bent the plot
   not him, dear
   marry when you love, dear
   and I will stand behind you
   but watch, too, the purse
   economy is all, dear
   but—let it be yours,

not theirs, the men
who bargain in the hall
for statecraft or the size of the estate.

Where else could Portia learn
that all that glisters is not gold?
There had to be a mother
in the house.

IN THE MARBLE ROTUNDA, BY A FOUNTAIN

A girl of ten tosses a penny,
aims for the upper bowl and misses,
the coin bouncing to the floor near my feet.
Hardly seeing me, she retrieves it,
and tries again.

I want to embrace her,
tell her that life gives us
second chances, even third.
She is skinny and tall, her hair
dishwater, her skin pale

but her step is light
her voice trills
and I want to lift her up
as she poises at the lip
of discovery, at the valley

of light and dark, heat and chill.
It's a journey she cannot imagine
despite all she can see
as she gazes ahead.

She gazes, though not for long,
then returns to her good life
where she dries the dinner dishes
as her mother's hands

stir in the sudsy sink
and they talk in low tones
of delicate things.

A FOREST

not a dark or hidden place
but a park, with great pines and spruce
and clearings among them where children play,

not the forest of Hansel and Gretel or the Black one
whose young men leave on quests, not knowing
they must return to flaxen-haired Helga

not the forest of nymphs and satyrs, where
magic is strong, music lurks in branches light and dark,
something cloven can jump at you from behind a tree

not that kind of forest

a forest with a glen, a zephyr,
sunbeams slanting with a holy light, no magic,
only children counting the needles of white pines

white pines fragrant in their palms
only children and angels
that forest

***

in the forest she turns and moves toward light
where angels dance, the sun glinting
through diaphanous bodies. Her arms

full of goldenrod, larkspur, and daisies
that never wilt, she glides along the edges,
sometimes in sun, sometimes in shadow. Maybe

the angels see her, maybe not, they are dancing.
She is dancing, too, slowly, in and out
along the sun-shade border, tossing flowers

now and then into the middle of the glade.
She twirls as the angels part to let her through,
arms raised, the flowers flowing around her, none falling.

SNOW AND SILENCE

The third eye sees all the secrets of the night,
the grappling, the dreaming,
the stars which blink us to sleep
or try to—

Some of us pace through a house lit only by snow
and in the blessed silence
we open our shirts to the third eye,
begging to be seen, and to see.

An Osprey

Perched on a high post, a silver fish
pinned in the talons of one foot,
the osprey stands guard.

Slowly, methodically, he dips
his beak into the head, nips
and pulls upright, a string of white flesh

in his mouth. He works his head
forward and back three times; then,
the flesh is gone.

He pauses, scans from left to right:
Whatever moves is in his eye.
Yards away, on another post,

where cross-planks can support it,
is the nest, and her white head
above its rough twig walls.

Whatever comes, he will protect her.
This fish does not matter.
There will always be others.

At ease for the moment,
he dips again into the flesh,
eats his way through the head,

one claw steady on the weathered post,
the other maneuvering his meal.
Gulls swoop by, sculling for scraps

but the osprey is a frugal eater,
letting little fall. This fish
can feed both him and her.

The morning sky is pure blue, the air still.
As I shift from one foot to the other,
I attract his eye. His wings lift, and I see

on the wrists the feathery eye-spots
meant to frighten me away.
He warns the air with four sharp cheeps,

musical, really, not rough at all.
It is enough. I go still,
though I do not leave.

They mate for life, I'm told, but her mate
floated up dead by the dock
two years ago, twisted in fishing line.

She sat on the post, waited
for another of their kind.
If she had died, he'd have waited.

That's how they do it,
these loyal birds, charged
by nature to go on.

Today as she sits, he feeds,
bite by bite, on his catch.
The head is gone, the tail

still splayed in the talon.
A pelican sails by, the osprey
flaps his wings twice, sharply.

From the far post his mate
begins to call. He will take
the rest of the fish to her

or he will finish it himself,
then soar away to get another.
Never mind. Selfish as he may seem,

eating first, he must fortify himself
for the long days of fishing for them all,
if not this mate, this brood, the next one,

husbandry
all he knows to do.

ABSENCE

in the Isabella Stewart Gardner Museum

Mary is everywhere
the boy, too, of course
but it's Mary here
in plaster or bronze or paint
Mary in homespun or velvet
Mary with crown or mantle
goldfinch or apple.

Where is the father?
Not he who sent the lily—
that was the easy part—
Where is the dad
who teaches the boy
to labor at the lathe
to honor his mother?
Where is he who
teaches the boy
to be a man?

Even when he appears, just once
here in these dark rooms, by Botticelli,
he is old, his curls rich with gray,
and he looks not out at us
but down
his only task
to give the boy away.

One Prayer

If I could make one prayer, it would be for Hilda
whose body is debated by doctors who declare
as they circle the bed that the red line peaks
the machine pumps air the bag fills yellow
and the brain is dead.

I would pray for Hilda as her husband waits
his hand hard on hers as the muscles waste.
Daily he knows that the bones come closer
but he will not sign, he will not sign.
What he feels is the hand of the girl he touched,
the hand of the woman who gripped his arm,
the flying hand of the pastry-maker,
the broth-spooner, seam-stitcher, singer of time.
Now, hand over hers, he will not sign.

Lawyers in the hall cite cases, expectations,
invoking the Doctrine of the Standard of Care,
and cost, always cost, insurance limitations,
machines, and space, for others waiting there . . .

In the doorway are the daughters, searching for their mother.
They step over wires, keep their bodies taut,
not to touch the machines or the one that was their mother.
They visit now on Tuesdays, the static of their loss
too hard for other days. Hands at their sides,
they bend to her forehead before they go.

Every morning the nurse brings a basin, wrings a cloth,
cleans around the eyes ears nostrils and the corners
of the mouth gums tongue, lubricates the lips,

wrings the cloth, strokes the neck shoulders armpits
between each finger, between each toe
croons *Hilda Hilda, are you in your skin,*
do you feel the sun, hear the shoosh of your breath,
do you know my hands on your breast on your feet
hush, Hilda, don't you cry
you'll go to heaven bye and bye.
Her hands wash Hilda as her hands wash the dead.
If she could make one prayer, it would be for Hilda.

Nana, Steadfast

Two men came for Wilson, leaving her
with the two small children.
Come home to us, her father said.
Come home and raise your children here.

He wouldn't let her go to work,
never let her husband
in the house again
never spoke his name.

Nor did the girl and boy.
To them he was dead and
they did not want to make her cry.
They were good children. Lucky, too,
because they were loved.

They would never know
what happened to their father.

Older, they began to wonder—
did the son take after him
did the daughter have his eyes—until

just weeks before their mother died,
the daughter asked at last:
"Ma, what happened?"

Nana pulled a picture from her dress.
"Your father," she said.
"He was so nice."

LAMENT AT LOW TIDE

for Bob

Drawn by the power
of their white vestments,
egrets convene
in the warm grass,
ghost-ships of the souls
gone before us.

Saturday morning there are two
who linger by the pool
during the frantic phone calls—
his mother in her leaving,
and his wife, her shepherd:
     No hurry, she says,
     take your time,
     leave slowly,
     though leave you must.
     I shall wait with you.

     Perhaps he'll see me here,
     know me as I know him
     and see him all the days,
     perhaps he knows me, too—

     not in the dreary ground
     where he stood with head bowed,
     clutching flowers that flash-freeze
     in the winter air

but in the other times, as when
the music plays or he
tastes my fine sauces.

Another bird comes but stays in the tree,
his father, gone so long
he does not want to come too close,
comes only to beckon his wife.
      There will be dancing, dear.
      I'll wait. As I have waited.

The egrets leave as the tide leaves,
and resume their quotidian duties,
what they do when they are not ghosts.
Landing far out in the shallows,
they dip into sea mud for crustaceans.
Sunday I count others,
six of them in the trees,
mangroves whipped bare by
the summer's hurricanes.
Six. My number. Those
who have gone before me.
One alone in the far tree
must be my girl, the senior soul,
gone so long, though so young.
These spirits abide for me
as I keep watch.

Monday just one. She
dips her beak into the pool,
sips, preens under feathers,
lifts her long neck into the
signature S, turns to east and west,
presenting her best side.

He leaves for Florida today
I will miss him
his mother wrote on her last day.

Solo now, gaining confidence,
she tries her just-fledged wings.
She has shed the bones sore with cold,
the weak lungs, the prickling skin.

Today she does not come.
Perhaps she will—after—
after wake and Mass, interment
and the rituals of consolation.

Perhaps then, feathers ruffing
in her lifted wings,
she will drift over the sea
as flights of angels
lead her to her rest
and perpetual light
shines upon her.

THIS IS A WOMAN'S HOUSE

An old house on an ocean bluff
a garden hoed and weeded
the table laid, an old house
with cupola and gambrel roof
porches crisp white.
Dormers look to the sea.

Lattice underneath the porches
keeps out all but the smallest creatures,
lets in the offshore breeze
to keep the wood dry.

Inside, one place is set for everyday,
the china sprigged in blue.
The pink, for Sundays, and
when the minister comes,
stays behind the corner glass.

This is a woman's house by the sea,
but she no longer waits. No one left
to wait for in the upstairs room
where the chair faces the window.
Sometimes when she sits there,
her needles working in her lap,

she lifts her eyes to the window.
A breath comes quicker.
It is habit, that is all.
Her eyes return to her work
and she rocks, as she always has,
the pine branch brushing against the glass.

This is a woman's house, the linens
folded in the drawers, the carpets swept,
a few asters in a bottle by the sink.
A pie cools in the window facing the hill
away from the predictable
unpredictable sea.

STARS: A GIFT

From an old pink bedspread,
the warp and woof worn soft,
and three wool blankets
spread on the living room floor,
he made me a bedroll.

He smoothed the layers together
with his warm hands
and folded, as explorers do,
the sides to the center,
overlapping generously,

and pinned them with four-inch blanket pins
he took from a cigar box
in the back of his top dresser drawer.
Boy Scout medals and other memories
clinked as his fingers rummaged.

He folded up the foot of the bedroll twelve inches,
tucked the ends in and pinned again,
the layers pierced and secured for my comfort
as I went to my first night under stars.

Make a bed of pine needles first, you'll be fine,
he said as his hands rolled my cocoon.
Look up through the branches, breathe deep.
I went bravely then, into that night.

Now he goes bravely, too.
I smell pine as I kneel
and touch my father's hands,

hands so cold in this stark room
as he goes to his nights in the stars.

BITTER IN MY MOUTH

Mother pulled all the weeds herself yesterday
as they used to do together,
as they did just this spring.

There is deep dish apple pie on the table,
but for supper she sets out bread and cold cuts.
"Make your own," she says.
She does not order us "Out of my kitchen, all of you!"
as she has done before.

I want to be home in the old way,
to be waited on, home to Mother.

This time I am the one
to reach out my hand and touch her arm.
Mugs of morning coffee between us,
her sorrow, not mine,
spreads across the breakfast table.

Later, she wakes from dozing on the couch
with gorge in her mouth. Startled,
she gasps, and acid rasps into her lungs.
Her lip quivers. We are both thinking
this is how it will be, but this time
I am here, I run toward the cough, hear
the wheeze of a burned bronchus, see her fear.

This time she gets up to the kitchen for water,
pours a spoon of Maalox. My mother
has always been cool in a crisis. But

one day she will be alone, he is already gone,
and the rest of us are visitors. I stand
by the sink, my hand on her shoulder,
a taste of something bitter in my mouth.

SURVIVORS

One small sack of groceries,
for one meal at a time,
maybe some cereal
for the mornings,
he stops at the market
each evening, later than usual,

goes home to one fork, one knife
flowers wilting in the living room,
a drink, the sports page, TV jumping
as he taps, taps the remote.
His head slides against the sofa;
he can't go up the stairs.

———————

She no longer waits
for the phone to ring
in her pocket at work.
That call has come and gone,
and now she has retired,
work too much to carry
along with sorrow.

Now she lets the dog in and out,
leans over to pull a weed. Inside
she strips paper from bathroom walls,
pulls up the rugs and starts over
with soap and swatches.
Movers store the piano for months.
The dog goes in and out.

What Jackie Said

Dying is not scary.
I was in the moment
no past, no future
all around me were talking, talking
    we're going to lose her
Mark was pacing, distraught
Jenny sobbing, *Mom, Mom*
I heard them say I
wasn't breathing
    ascites at the diaphragm
I saw them working so hard
the ones who felt in charge
I saw the others crying
their red faces
and I knew I couldn't
leave them on their own.
I was not afraid.

GODSON BY PROXY

Had I not flown to Boston when he was taken to the Floating Hospital
where in decades past children were taken away
from the sweltering city to heal in the fresh sea air
where Danny was taken for surgery to correct Tetralogy of Fallot—

Had I not rocked him against my breast as I walked
the now-solid ground of the Floating, where miracles are daily made—
had I not glimpsed beneath his shirt the barreling ribs
and the sucked-in sternum as he tried so hard to gulp
oxygen enough to grow

into the little boy he had been meant to be,
had I not finally flown—though not in time for the ceremony of
   water and the spirit—
I would have missed him forever. They hadn't said
how frail he was, how tinged with blue

how little he had thrived since
his newborn photo had come in the mail.
I had been sad but not alarmed, had told my sister, his mother
they do this surgery every day for babies smaller than Danny

I knew they could repair it all—
the hole in his heart, the narrowed artery, the aorta's double bad
   connection—

until, until I watched him breathe.

The Floating Hospital for Children, Tufts University, New England Medical Center
Tetralogy of Fallot—a complex of four malformations in the newborn heart

The Plagues, the Ghosts

Here they are again, not with buboes swollen to exploding,
not with rats—
at least none we can see—

the microbes are at war again, marching through towns like
pipers, drawing

the children from schools and who knows where they will end up,
febrile, dehydrated.

Ghosts from times past collect along the roadsides.
One by one

they take our children by the hand, put an arm around a
shoulder, and begin
to whistle softly—

it is not the wind we hear, busy with pills and poultices, broth
and blankets
all we know to do.

FOR MY BROTHER, NEVER DYING

he would not let us say the word
I'm living my life! he said
as his body ate itself from the inside out

from the wheelchair he leered and whistled
as his wife vamped before him
slapping the spoons on her bare thigh
shoulders a-shimmy to the music
living, he said, *my life*
as he raised his glass and winked

they severed some nerves in his spine
to stop the pain from interrupting
his living-not-dying

it would be ugly, he knew the first day
and I haven't been that bad a guy
this brother

who stepped from the golf cart
pissed blood on a tree
then drove the ball 300 yards
a port pumping drugs in his chest

I swore I would wear a red dress
black is no color for this man

THE PALMS

Mangroves sway and all the palms click,
each in its own voice as the breeze freshens,
rehearsing for the storm to come.

Behind me, tall heavy-bladed palms in a clump so tight
they clack against each other, rise higher than this balcony,
so thick they bar the wind. My feet, propped on the railing, feel
  only a wisp.

Below me, fans of palmetto wave back and forth like the ones
clutched on sticks on hot Sundays in a Southern church as the
  congregants intone
"When the Roll Is Called Up Yonder I'll Be There."

High above the house, date palms rustle, their fronds rock
as they did in Jerusalem, as I shall do this Sunday here in Florida,
as the family will do in the cold north,

taking home one long leaf apiece, to bend into a cross
to tuck into a corner of a dresser mirror. Last year's is brittle now,
pale, no longer the bright green promise of renewal.

Palms—a talisman—of sacrifice, salvation—come down true
  through the ages.
As we stand while the whole long Passion is read again,
do we really still know what it means?

Don't throw old palms in the trash, mother said.
Dad will burn them behind the garage. That smell is incense rising.

Snowflakes

Another day's snow begins.
Against the dark cedars
each crystal splays its fingers like no others.

More thickly now they fall,
down and down,
and now I say it's snowing,
the flakes en masse, indistinguishable
like notes in the concert hall.

By this window wall
where warmth slips
through Thermopane
gravity slows, and a few flakes
float upward along the glass.
They rise up, touched by mortal heat.

V. Sing Anyway

ALONE ON SUNSET ROCK

I. Spring

Proprietor
the beaver glides
around the point, outlining
his estate. Out of
my sight he
swirls
and swims
the arc again.
His eye lands hard on my chest
alone here on this
rock.

II. Summer

A small boat
trolls around the point
lines extended into deep weeds.
Man and wife turn their hat brims
toward the sunset. They wave.
I wave. A last skier
whizzes past, arm
upraised.

III. Fall

One loon left
adult too large, serene
to be this season's juvenile.

He swims around the point where
lake floor drops, underwater grasses
shelter fish, young fish, who cannot get away.
On his slow circle he dives and rises,
dives and rises where my eye
just swept the surface.
He looks away.

IV. Winter

I look back
from the silent ice
toward Sunset Rock, its blush
granite brushed with snow, its face
worn glacier smooth and rumbled onto my shoreline.
No creatures in the stillness here but me,
no wake, no tracks, just this:
another kind of power—
to walk on water.

THE QUESTION IS SAFETY

in damp reeds by the side of the road
brown fuzzed stalks shelter me
and mud sucks at my knees

as I crouch safely in the ditch
in the ditch—in the low place
damp with standing water

where algae breed and molder
where the bodies of insects decay
where the wet roots of cattails are all

that does not putrefy—
in the ditch is safety
from the clarity of sunlight

and the winnowing of dead things
in the western breeze
until winds from the south blow up

into torrents of sudsing and rinsing
as wind whips reeds on their backs
and lightning floods every secret place

SHE THINKS SHE IS A RIVER

Egrets lift long wet legs from her shallows,
their white bodies gray shadows
as they rise in the half-light of morning.
What live in her are bottomfish
nosing in the muck,
working the life of the river.

Once in a while a pike leaps the surface
silver-finned in a passing shade
and she knows she is a river,
mire and beauty together
deep and running in her natural course,
running with burden and blessing,
breaking the banks when safety is too much.

She floods both enemies and innocents,
and the channel is never the same.
Some places are sluggish still—
she knows it is always that way.
Some places surge onward, free and sure.

NOVEMBER, ALL SOULS

In the solemnity of incense
we pray for them, as if our prayers will lift them
through circles of eternal absolution.
Each year we pray as the ledger grows—
our souls, so many who have left us here
in the known world, imagining theirs for which
we are not ready.

Perhaps they need our help to be absolved, though of what
must infant Danny be absolved confounds me, godmother,
witness to the rite of purification, or my daughter
with her straight As and music and shine

or the old ones, Dad and Nana, who had years enough
on the ledger to have done whatever penance for their good lives.
What need have they of absolution? What need have they of me
except to remember? Even Peter, neither innocent nor wise,
eaten in the fullness of a blazing life, what need has he
to be absolved of joyful life?

And yet we pray, imploring them
to shepherd us and calm our fear,
as we pray for absolution, theirs
and ours.

I SING ANYWAY

Dirt grinds into my calves as
I sit cross-legged in the garden
cutting soil and roots into cubes
careful of the thin green stems of zinnias.

I bury each chunk in the friable earth,
press the soil like a silk-bordered
blanket around each stem
fighting the flower's desire
to lean over, to lie down
in the dirt and rest.

I sing in the garden, though
all around me are dying.
Pinch back mums, snap off
the wilted heads of marigolds.
I rub my face with the
pungent gold of raucous blooms,
lick the gritty earth under my nails,
rub it with teeth and tongue.
        Morning has broken, like the first morning . . .
        Blackbird has spoken, like the first bird . . .

I stand up, dizzy in the sun heat,
lean against the hot brick of the garage.
Blood rushes into my stiff legs,
drains from heart and head.
I sing anyway.

How To Be Alone

Sit by a lakeside window.
Yes, just one, no,
I'm not waiting for anybody.
A hamburger, please. I guess
I'll have a beer. Why not.

Look away from two fishermen
who watch me. One says
You look like a woman I know.
Her name is Sharon. I laugh, say,
there are clones of me everywhere.

A hummingbird comes to the window feeder,
darts away. That is how it is done:
Move in quickly, eat, drink, do
what you have to do. Leave the watchers
with your ruby throat
and the whisper of your name.

Glaciers and Women

This is the Ranger speaking: We are turning into Hopkins fjord, can go no farther as the harbor seals have pups on ice floes close to the glacier.

Pups, floes, lovers, children—
they break apart from us—
calving with a great crack

to plummet into the green sea.
Nothing subtle
about their departure.

Meanwhile
snows pile on and press us into ice
with simple gravity.

Sometimes
we advance again, creeping forward
toward the sea

until
from our undersides,
we calve again into white thunder.

THE *MESABI MINER* APPEARS ON LAKE SUPERIOR

Here with nothing special going on
this warm sunny day
as pines and firs and birches
bend not at all in a breeze barely there

a man-made thing one thousand feet long
slides smoothly, silently into my view
loaded I know with 62,000 tons of iron ore
and all the diesel fuel it needs
to slide over the brow of the world toward the Soo
to Gary, Detroit, Cleveland, Lorain.

Who are you whose infinite faculties
made this thing? Whoever you are
who sat with ink and slide rule
sheets of paper gridded into squares
with mathematics and your imagination
one late-burning lamp

to thee I sing. You,
whoever you are, you
are a wonder of the world.

Cold November Morning

leaning
from a balcony
in my fat
bathrobe, tea

frosting in my cup
I squint
through cedars
into a bright ball of sun

a hot glare
torches the ripples
on a Great Lake
and I am warm

THOUGH STUCK IN TRAFFIC, I AM NEVER WITHOUT POETRY

in homage to WCW

so much slow traffic through
road construction barrels

on Cedar Avenue in Apple Valley
a Dodge 4x4 beside me

balanced upon the rim
of the pickup truck's bed

a cage filled with white chickens,
heads turning in the breeze

one feather alights on my windshield
there's no rainwater on this sunny day

did I mention, depend on it,
the truck is red

In the Hotel Bar

I met an officer of the Third Reich. Eighty now,
he was not remorseful, he was not triumphant.
He laughed and expounded, sure of his audience.

His father, a diplomat, had meant him
for the law. His grandfather, who could
see war coming, sent him instead to the
Brandenburg Military Academy, knowing
the military would have advantages over law.
His was the first class to graduate
after Hitler came to power.

Near the end of the war
he went behind enemy lines in Russia.
He didn't say why.
On a mission? Escape?

He has bullets in his back,
one by his spine, pinching a nerve.
At the end, he said, the Germans
shot off his leg midthigh.
He didn't say why.

> I asked if he had met Hitler. Yes,
> just before the end, March 1945,
> in the center of a long dark tunnel.

During three hours we sat together in the hotel bar
Herb talked nonstop, smiling, telling some stories over and over.

I caught the crest of a breath to ask about Hitler's end,
caught another to ask what would have happened

if Germany had won the war.
     Well, he said,
     we would have gone into countries—
     as rulers.
It was the only time he slowed down.

CHANGE WE NEED

with a change
with a change of deity to pine trees or palm
no image, no holy book to insist in triumph
        mine is better than yours

with a change of deity to rock or water, something
        easy for everyone
        maybe air would be best

walls would be no more than walls
the sands could shift without significance
the seas rock back and forth and blue

sweeping would be done on floors, no armaments involved
burkhas could be sliced into bandages
vestments could be stapled onto furniture . . .

think of it

no change would come to strawberries or lamplight
the mountains would yield their snow
the grass its silken touch against the foot

IN THE TIME OF THE CHERRY BLOSSOMS

In Kyoto
in morning twilight
the mimosa tree
glows by the wooden gate

Behind the old house
Hiroko hangs
the early morning laundry
looks to the sky
and goes inside
to brew the tea

In Tokyo
in midafternoon
Kumiko and her coworkers
walk steadily west
in their navy skirts and weskits
and high heels

In Sendai
Mari climbs a small hill
lifting Naoki to her back
just in time

At Fukushima
steam rises
laden
with cesium

At Kiyomizu
high on a hill above Kyoto
the temple stands
now as in centuries past
its forty pilings
each a mighty tree
unshaken

Here the *sakura* will blossom
veiling the hillside
veiling every hillside in Japan
delicate petals swaying
as the people masked and silent
stand in line for water

Paris

I. Cathedrals

It is all
a matter of
art
engineering
and
the search
for God.

II. Monuments

It is all
a matter of
pride
and
power
personal
and national.

III. Luxembourg Gardens

Perhaps
it is all
a matter of
beauty
and rest.

AMERICAN MEMORIAL

Not the bronze equestrian, sword raised,
tassels flying from his helmet.
Not the seated queen, accepting
from her kneeling emissary
a hemisphere of gold and silver.

Our heroes we salute by their names
carved one by one, first name, middle, last,
    into a dark wall that cleaves the ground—
    onto seats in an Allegheny field and slabs by the walls of war—
    onto the sides of two silver acres in the city as water falls into
    deep pools—

where on this Sunday morning, blue and clear,
three thousand names fill the airwaves
from sea to shining sea.

November Gale, Lake Superior

Seven women bring a weekend's food—
lasagna and salad, bread and wine,
breakfasts, a pie, more wine,
and a pot of wild rice soup
riding in the back seat.

We hike no river's cliff, retreat
from ledge rocks wet with spray
as the seiche of Superior
rocks and rises into surf as wild
as on the North Atlantic.

By windows we watch birches bend
and cedars sway as our talk
bends and sways—a baby this year,
another wedding next, and all
the quotidian moments of thirty years together.

High winds outside, high spirits inside.
Around the table friends encircle
griefs and glories past. Today
all is well.

Deal the cards.

*seiche: a temporary oscillation in the water level of a lake,
esp. one caused by changes in atmospheric pressure.

POEM OF WONDER

There is a moment just before the wave
breaks over the rock, when I can gauge

—if my eye is quick—
the height from crest to trough.

But mostly I just watch, suspended
longer than the wave suspends,
                                        and wonder

about water and wind, power and oscillation
                                        about the distance

between truth and falsehood, joy and pain,
love and its awful trough, indifference.

WORRY

like a gray cloud on the horizon,
settles into my view just out of reach.
There is much to worry about—the world
the children, their children, their present and future
and what I can do about it
besides sit here on a dock
on a cool northern lake
and turn toward the west
where a few shards of light break through

*

taking a break from worry
you settle down beside me
as I study gray water, gray clouds

like a con man prestidigitating
you slip the cards out of sight
invite a pale light to flutter down over us
obscuring the dark sky

A Secret

How shall we be together
this secret and I?

Can we bear the bonds
of the small, tight space between us?

Will we nudge elbows and
smile our secret smiles

feel something precious
warm us?

Can we contain it?
Will we begin to glow?

*

Once I
utter it, it
isn't secret
anymore. It's
mine and yours
and you will
speak it
as you will
and I
must let it go.

*

Word leaks out,
some whisper
among themselves,

privy to an indiscretion,
triumph, or despair.
The air sizzles

for a time, then settles
until the pressure cooks
and must release.

SCREEN SAVER

History passes by at six-second intervals
travels
  visits
    holidays
      the spring garden
        a young elk
          favorite aunt
            the Badlands
              Charlie on the Alpine Slide.

The screen dims after three minutes
I can hardly see
  the egret's long white neck
    bending into mud flats at low tide
    or mother at ninety with cake.

Castles, flumes, eruptions, children
all go by before me as I wait
  for inspiration, until
    the screen, reaching
      its limit of suggestion
        goes dark.

LOOK NO FURTHER OVER MY LIFE

all is calm except the music
let hubris, let hamartia go
let no princes die
on the cusp of act five
don't sit still
get up, get dancing

Paint Me

Paint me in music
of a century past,
try the long Eighteenth as it slips
over the cusp from Mozart
to Beethoven,
or better,

go right to Chopin.
His loves are my loves
his etudes my diligence
his arpeggios my delight—
yes, make it Chopin.

Don't bother
with thunderous chords
that will bring them to their feet
crying *Brava, Brava.*
It's not the great voices

I wish to inhabit.
It's the spirits
that speak to them
at twilight and dawn
when everything is possible.

GLORIA MUNDI

after Jane Kenyon

Let the sun hold on to the top of the ridge.
Let the city nod in shadow.
Let bells go silent, the lake turn to silk,
the rocks settle in by the waterside.
A dragonfly rests on a leaf of yarrow.
Its parchment shell slips slowly off,
the last of the sun dries the new one.

Let the blackflies be satisfied
and a loon sit low in the water.
Let the dark wait above us,
the clouds become rose and hover.
For now let the turning hold.
Let the moment of passage be.

VI. EVERYTHING BEAUTIFUL

BEACH WALK AT HAPPY HOUR

Tide's in now. Burned shoulders
scratch against my shirt.
I scoop sea water into my palms
and sip the salt that tastes of home.

Great swells slide up and over rocks
where barnacles and mussels collect in crevices.
Ebbing waters will desert them in the night.
Where do they find comfort?

Climb a granite boulder, the only one
higher than the tide, my knees
scraping crystals from its surface.
Look out to the sea and sky

as an orange sun burns the atmosphere to blue,
calms the waves that pounded me all day.
Sails float like spirits
on a band of haze at the horizon.

Below me a jellyfish rises.
Its cellophane edges ruffle in the waves
around its blood-dark heart.
Everything beautiful has its sting.

PERIWINKLES

A child, I suppose, has lined them up
and left them here in a row
like the desks at school—
five periwinkles plucked from the tide pool.
They stand, as if waiting for the bell,

along a seam of milky quartz in the black basalt
of this rocky shore. Periwinkles,
their twilight blue drying to gray,
their soft, elastic bodies shrinking inside curled shells
as the tide recedes and the sun arches.

I want to intervene, to wet them with salt water
I could carry in my hands, or knock them
into a lingering wave. Then I see a pod
extend from one shell, plant itself
a millimeter outward and tease itself along.

It is the smallest one. Again it reaches
forward, and again, until it is at the edge.
I think it will lean and tumble
into the pool below. It does not.
Its sure foot stretches over the edge,

sucks onto the vertical face
and pulls the shell over,
one deliberate step at a time,
inching down the precipice
patiently, as all good work is done,

patiently, and with a trust
that instinct and the lure of water
are the proper guides.
I look up and see
that the other four have followed,

at the edge now and over,
a column of creatures stepping
smartly down the ledge
until each shell slips under rockweed
into the damp dark, into the place
that leads to home.

FAITH

Over
the barren expanse of the Great Plains watching the Missouri as it
loops and loops, I think of Lewis and Clark and young Sacajawea,
paddling upstream into an American faith in a way to the ocean,
a way across a continent to a limitless horizon for trade and the
imagination.

It had to be
a faith of great proportions to draw them through the days of
desolate space, which even now, two hundred years later, is empty
of everything but taupe-colored flats and hills and a few wrinkles
of tributaries making their way to the Missouri. How did they
keep on?

Long past
the blue of the river swollen behind Garrison Dam, the land rises
darkly into deep green firs. Clouds appear, trapped where there
could be mountains. Imagine the sight of these high clouds, the
glimpse of a forested ridge! If not the undulant hills of the Blue
Ridge or Smokies, at least the promise of enfolding arms to break
the loneliness of the open range, however magnificent its sky, and
lead them to the sea.

And yet
these were not Appalachia's upholstered hills but the august
upthrusts of the Rockies, a barrier more daunting than the open
range and the insistent muddy river's eastward current. The only
way was over.

Aloft

we do not need to bargain for Shoshone horses to climb into the
Bitterroots. We will not have to eat our dogs to survive through
snow. Our feet will not bleed nor our fingers freeze. We soar
across the Continental Divide, its sharp upheavals of the Earth's
crust. We buckle our seatbelts, put our seatbacks and tray tables
into an upright and locked position, sail over the Columbia,
between the snowy peaks of the Cascades, and glide down
through clouds, delivered.

Waiting for Love

now the waiting
begins anew

on a higher, sweeter
plane, the delicate ding

of the doorbell, hello
of the phone, announcing

a venture
into *terra incognita,*

that far-off land
one thinks

never to have
glimpsed again

I hear it now, faintly
in the damp night

in the humming
of the wires,

the click of crickets
all around me

I sense it
fingers, eyes, tongue

and the tang of summer sun
my skin thrumming

like a bell
that might ring

Pinecliff Woman Saves Dog

headline in The Mountain-Ear
Nederland, Colorado

In a reservoir high in the Rockies
in water as cold as the glacier
somebody's dog got tangled
in a weir underwater intended for fish

beneath the Continental Divide
the Pinecliff woman plunged in
no dog a stranger to her
no dog too gone for her, my girl

    did she kick off her boots
    did she throw down her coat
    did she toss her keys to the sand
    could she keep her feet free of the net

Yes, she untangled the dog that day
as the children watched stony from shore
knowing the peril that she forgot
in March in the mountains

at nine thousand feet
in the cold and the wet
in the mountains in March

my Pinecliff woman, crooning
to the dog stretched out on the shore

THE TABLE

She drops the string bag
with her greens for supper
onto the blue tile table by the door.

He had brought it home
one day from the thrift store.
Though they had no room for it,

she liked it, really, and praised him
for his find. He was so rarely
domestic that she'd have loved it

even if it were ugly, a judgment
this table just barely avoids.
Its legs are uneven, it wobbles,

the surface is rough. The artist
must have been a novice, as
many of the sharp tiles

of the mosaic rise
out of the plaster.
Nevertheless, she kept it

when he left,
put it on the patio
of her new place.

Not that she wanted memories of him.
Not that she would ever be without
memories of him.

The Babies Tell Us

The babies tell us
  where we are
  where we're going
  where we've been.

The babies mark our lives
  even when
  they're not babies
  anymore.

When they're not babies
  anymore
  they're still
  our babies.

We go to them to mark
  where we are
  where we're going
  where we've been.

Even in their absences they tell us
  who we are
  who we were
  who we are still becoming.

Bob and the Graves

On the approach of every holiday
and on the day of each remembrance
he arrives with clippers, knife,

something beautiful wrapped in foil.
On his knees he clips away encroaching grass,
brushes off detritus from both stones—

his wife, and my girl he never knew.
He carries water, snips stems,
leaves something beautiful behind.

PROPHECIES

I don't make them anymore
not about the weather—
I gave that up first.
I wonder when the leaves will turn
but I don't guess the day
or what the tea leaves say.

For the children it was my job
to imagine the next week, next month,
their years ahead and how I
could prepare them.
I did it reasonably well
but now they have to do it for themselves.

I could prophesy my future
but that's easy—I'll pay taxes
yet again this year—and
there aren't so many other avenues
nor are the choices especially salubrious.
Best not to invite foresight.

Take a break from prophecy.
Sit in the blaze of sunset
this sunset, its rose, its plum, its apricot.

BOB IN THE GARDEN

makes order from profusion,
geraniums spaced by ruler,
an edge precisely dug. He brings out
the level to straighten the stake
the birdhouse sits on.

Before Bob there was design, perennials opened in sequence,
ginger poppies bloomed beside blue iris,
and the colors of each season repeated around corners
though the roots of lawngrass reached into the beds
undeterred most days—I chopped them
when I thought of it but couldn't manage
the long loops of black edging—one end down and backfilled
and   *sproing*   the other end curled up
until I tossed the whole business behind the garage.

The garden has order and clean lines where once
peonies drooped over catmint, the heads of echinacea curled their
  long stems
out from under the new tree toward the sun,
while last year's alyssum popped up between nasturtiums.
Liatris, lupine, lychnis, and lobelia—whatever was new—waved
  among the roses
and not a few weeds luxuriated in the dark places under foliage.

We are weed free and clean edges now, species grouped in threes.
It's beautiful. Still, he calls me when it's time to place the colors.

New England Poem

The train cuts through granite hills
west of Boston, passes old stations,
hip-roofed and wide-eaved, then enters
the thick brown woods splashed everywhere
with arches of forsythia. Overhead

the maples bud into red froth
at their crowns, and birches glow
with the chartreuse of newborn
catkins dripping from their branches.
A man in a red cap fishes
in a brook edged with stones.

Stones everywhere. A wall,
old and dark and mossy,
follows the curve of a hill
as if set by the Old Neighbor himself.

This is my New England,
heart of the ancient forest
trees in white flower
trees in pink flower
and somewhere the arbutus trails,
the mayflower of this acid soil.

By Worcester's huge railyard
brick smokestacks rise from
factories grimed with age, their windows
row on row of clouded glass.
Piles of railroad ties leach creosote,
rusted rails stack up in traprock

and we roll again through fields and towns
churches everywhere,
Italian, Ukrainian, Pilgrim—
a white steeple, a Norman crown.

The train climbs into foothills
as the rock closes in again.
Tracks in the granite show
where dynamite blew these hills
into tunnels just wide enough
for rails and progress.

It's the fashion this year
to read history, feisty Adams,
benevolent Ben, the Great Father himself
and the great year, '76, all in bright covers
in airports, and even on railroad platforms
here in my Massachusetts

where in that time and this place
Colonel Henry Knox, according to the story,
towed with oxen over mountains,
through forests not yet cleared for homesteads,
through forests without roads,

towed through ice and blizzard
the cannons of Ticonderoga
while Washington waited,
camped above Boston
where tea was poured from sterling.

Henry Knox, on his way to blow
the Redcoats out of Boston,
camped with his cannon
on the common of my hometown.

On my way to my hometown
I sip tea by a train window,
look down a rock-pocked slope
into a silver pool, into a forest floor
deep with leaves from last fall
and the one before and the ones before that.

All the signs of home are here—
a footpath emerging along the rills and rapids
of a west-running brook, a plowed field,
a weathered skiff on a narrow pond,

where yellow larches glow,
fiddleheads unfurl,
and in a swamp
great round leaves open
like fans in a summer church.
Rain spatters, we slow for a passing freight
and descend toward the Connecticut,
where, retreating from the muskets
of pioneers laying claim

to the river's rich bottomlands,
Metacomet's band, already
driven from their seashore lands,
ended their days in King Philip's Stockade.

The whistle blows as we enter Springfield
past a bright new factory by another rippling brook.
The Limited, rumbling on to the west without me,
will be on time, as time unfolds
in the Massachusetts woods.

TO LEAP OVERBOARD WITH AUDEN

for Julie

In spring they jump right to it, brave squadrons,
caps tossed in the air, jobs or no jobs in the air
and they must leap, as we all have done,
whether they have looked or not
whether they can see a spot
firm enough to land. It is a leap
let no one tell you it's a step
the fall is sharp, the air sizzles
there is no place secure enough to land.

The powers who have promised you stability and skill
a solid future when you finish each apprenticeship—
the powers know they lie, but they do not want to frighten you
new squadrons must arrive to take your place
and so they call on Auden to say "Look
if you must, but you will have to leap"

therefore keep on leaping
land only for awhile
keep on leaping
and you will learn to fly.

A Meditation on Retirement: My Daughter Worries I'll Be Bored

I've done my duty and I'll do more
I see it coming and I step right up—

you needn't worry—but now that I
have time to reconnoiter

I'd like to get to the head of the line
and claim the time and soundless space

to give back to myself a bit
of what I've spent elsewhere

I'd like to give myself some time to sit
with a cup and a book by a window or

find a place to climb up rocks where I must cling to trees
to hold my ground as water tumbles in eternal order

I'd like to hum to myself or sing out loud
I won't be bored or useless—

and you can be sure of this—
sitting still, I shall be most alive.

MY POEM TO THE PRAIRIE

I.
That first time around the curve of Lake Michigan
north out of Chicago, the land opened, the sky opened
(no hills, no hills anywhere)
I drew in a great breath, impressed as I was supposed to be
by scope, largesse of land, and amber waves of the Great
   Midsection of America

but there was nothing to hold onto, no place to rest my eyes
everywhere I looked the land dropped away, off the edge into air
       no sea before, no mountains behind
        years and years atilt on dry land.

Still I ache for hills, something blue-green, purple, even smoky to
  enfold me
to build a fence around the problem of geography

what hills can do, provide a frame of reference

II.
the seaside is my native place
an old house with a widow's walk, white railing
trap door creaky, unused for years   a chair by the window
waves slap the shore, the oven is still warm
this house will stand for another two hundred years

a sea gull settles on an upthrust boulder, looks to sea, unruffled
egrets lift from the shallows, feathers ruffing in the air of departure
an osprey dives and rises, a silver fish in its squared talons

out where the color deepens, lobster buoys sway in the ocean swells
a hurricane approaches, periwinkles cling, march without trepidation

III.
I did not know so long ago that
grass could whisper
waves will ripple through grain
fields rock in an August storm
I did not know that hope
is lost as quickly here
as on the sea, all hands down
as dawn breaks in a silver sky

IV.
the seaside is my native place, its rocky caverns
call me even now from the prairie,
this sea of sod where I push roots
deep down to an aquifer of new affection
fed by rivers and rain into pools enclosed by birch and pine
instead of dunes, no dunes anywhere

still, my place now, harvest or defeat, my place

Portrait of Grace at Nine, Lake Superior

She listens to the warnings about rocks, they are rough, will scrape your knee, they look solid but some rocks wobble when you step on them, stay close, don't set your feet on rocks that are wet, wet rocks are slippery, you could fall into the cold lake and get too cold in your tiny body before we could pull you out, keep both feet on dry rocks all the time, I am spoiling her fun, I can tell, by the patience with which she tilts her head and waits, she is used to that.

I watch her step carefully at first, her feet learning the long basalt ledge, and then she leaps a little, and her feet know, they hold her up, they balance her, and she is off leaping from boulder to boulder over deep seams and rock pools, out of sight. Busy watching her brother, whose feet have not yet learned, I see that I can't see her anymore, I hurry, not leaping, in her direction.

There she is. Her little seat fitted to a perfect rock, her back to me. Feet planted on the dry edge just above the water's splash, chin in hand, elbows on knees, ponytail still. She looks out over the lake to the horizon in the perfect solitude I remember, the perfect dream.

As You Are Forty

for Stephanie

I remember the summer day I held you on my lap
in front of the TV, your new head slumped sideways
on my flowered jumpsuit, I was so skinny then

and someone took a picture of us for posterity,
watching the man step onto the moon and
nothing since has been the same.

Nana saw the horseless carriage, the trenches, the airplane,
the famous Influenza, and the years that Roared,
though poets spoke of Wastelands—

Mother made it through the Crash, the Bomb, the Reds,
acquiring appliances and pearls, the big house
on Ohio Avenue where we lay under summer stars, a golden family—

Me, I vaguely remember duck-and-cover,
mine was the Torch passing, the Great Society,
Rosa and Gloria, then assassins, Tet, the break-in—

You, you were born to an extra-terrestrial age
wired, wireless, and in a Cloud
you will see, oh—what more you will see.

THE LUPINES ALONG HIGHWAY 61

Twelve years it took her
and now is the time. Yes,
she can do it all herself
though it will not be easy. Still,

the lilt of freedom
in her voice as she
called from the highway
with the kids and without him.

She noticed the deep blue of the summer sky, the puffs of white clouds,
the intense greens of the grass, the birch, the maples, and the
  endless forest.
She noticed the deep green of the pines along Lake Superior,
and she noticed the lupines, whole banks of indigo standing straight
even as the breeze freshened from the lake.

The Lupines! she exclaimed as she walked in our door.
Before today she would not have noticed the lupines.

FACEBOOK POST FROM TRICIA

I was mugged on my street tonight

I read with my morning tea

Mom, don't read this

As if.

by two big kids brandishing

me in Florida, she in Oakland

their shoulders, like Marlon Brando

blue sky, water, all you expect

I'm OK, convinced them

on vacation except for this post

I didn't have anything on me

palm trees sway as palm trees do

no money, no wallet

egret splays tail feathers in green grass

walking home from a friend's

lifts stick legs

after the Grammys

sets down thin rubber toes

I'm a teacher, I said

I watch the bird watch me

leave me alone

                    wait for dawn on the Pacific

told them to move on. They did.

                    send my reply by email and text:

Take back the night, Oakland!

                    I MUST BE YOUR FIRST CALL
                    THIS MORNING.

THE TELEPHONE

It was the second accident we saw that day—
the first a rollover,
the second
an hour later
a fiery crash—
that rubbed raw the nerve
so long scarred over.

A Hyundai slammed
a once-red MINI Cooper
into a semi
coming downhill.
The MINI charred to gray.
The truck's cab as well.
A bent hood
on the Hyundai.
Road closed six hours
to clean up.

All day
I hear a phone ring
somewhere.
All night
I wake,
my hand
reaching for it.

Rogue River Run

They could hit the canyon wall with
all the force of the insistent river.
A helmet would hardly help,
nor would holding my breath,

nor supplications to the mountain,
the gorge, the pebbles beneath,
the black bear that came
to the edge last night for trout.

Nothing can move the river
to be careful as it holds
the ones I love
in its grasp.

*

I come through the rapids arms up,
sailing like an athlete or a child who is fearless
though I left childhood behind years ago.

Eddied out now in the shallows by a forested hill
I can climb to the meadow above
or swim in the river's deep pool.
I can fish or float, weave reeds
or leap from a ledge.

There are rocks
downriver
but I am here
in blue water.

CLEAN YOUR CLOSETS NOW, SHE SAID

Do not think
        to leave the sorting
        to your daughters.

If they had wanted
        that old stuff
        they would have
        asked for it by now.

If there were treasures
        you'd have hocked them
        or given them away already.

Clean your closets now.
        Bestow the things you love
        on those you love. Recycle
        what you can. Bonfire the rest.

A trash truck is backing up next door.
No way to leave a legacy.

What We Leave Behind

money, poems, drawers of photos, scarves, forks, some things
  useful, some loved
we leave them to it, all the sorting, they can't just set a match to it
we leave them lessons learned, wisdom if they care to apprehend it

why can't you remember the good things, we say
and they do, though they won't admit it till we're old and feeble
they'd rather tease, accuse us, laughing at
how cautious we were and how they got around us—
the ladder to the back porch, for instance, a forbidden drive down
  Riverdale Road—

until we're old, we do not tell them how we slept all night in the
  dewy grass
at the end of the driveway, the front door too far away

so much we cannot tell across the generations
sins and scares we do not wish to leave behind
though we could have laughed together

As Long as We Don't Fight It

In twilight shadows a tanker's lights skim the steel-gray surface
of Lake Superior, and whitecaps rock to the shore. The ship,
huge and ponderous in port, slides now along the horizon,

not fighting the power of the lake, but not subdued.
A young gull walks the sand this way, until he sees me.
Wind lifts his feathers; he veers toward the safety of water.

He does not need the green light of the marina blinking behind him
to signal the point between safety and danger. Only boats need that
and creatures still fighting, still trying to understand.

Here at north latitude forty-seven degrees, the summer light
still spills this late over the hills behind me, slipping under the lake's
black clouds. Superior rocks back and forth, doing its work

as the ships do
as the gulls do
as we all do
taking order where we get it
taking comfort where it comes.

A CHILDHOOD

in the pointed shadow of my house I played house
imagined being grown-up and beautiful and loved
for a wild spirit I did not have then or now

Mother calls from the doorway
and I am sad to put away the afternoon's wild spirit, rue the
  moment of loss
but the wild spirit waits, never leaves, it waits
in the shadow of my house
in the dark behind the garage
in the open sea beyond the backyard trees

*

white horses gallop in little squares all over the wallpaper
you had to get up close to see that they were horses, not abstractions
you had to believe they could gallop out of those squares

(horses! how did she choose horses, white on beige
a neutral backdrop, yes, but horses at full gallop in their squares
in my mother's living room)

answering the phone, tied by its cord
to the Governor Winthrop desk in that room of Colonial perfection,
piecrust table, porcelain lamp, beveled mirror

I studied horses and squares, spirit and limit
and never understood a single thing about my mother's spirit

*

gravel in my knees marks my childhood,
the marks embedded still

the gravel of Homestead Avenue
or the bark of the tree down the hill

that I came to know without brakes
I feel today my father's arms lifting me, my mother's cheek

*

a traprock wall came to buttress the base of the hill
between us and the empty lot below
and we had no more gullies in the backyard
where boats could sail, where rain could carve channels
into soft dirt where no roots could hold

hauling rock, sweating through his white T-shirt
and throwing it off his pale thin chest, my father
fit the granite faces into each other, tipped them back
to hold the dirt around them, a true Yankee
businessman about the building of his wall

no more slip-sliding through sluices
trees were planted, tomatoes, too,
the backyard leveled and tamed
leaving us nothing to do
but leap from the wall

*

always at Christmas the same number of boxes apiece for the five
   of us
though mother's perfect penmanship could not be
disguised on tags no matter how she tried

*

supper waiting, I ask *Where's Daddy?*
Probably getting fired! her sputtered answer
and I saw bonfire and a stake and the saints,
could not grasp why she was angry,
not sad or scared as I was
until he came in whistling
couldn't happen, couldn't ever happen

we were lucky, always free to fancify,
never had to face all the things
I later had to face that I could face because
I was lucky

SOLSTICE SEASON

early morning dark
illuminated
by fresh snow

the brief blue hour
of twilight
far north

no other time
is the light just so
there must be snow

in blue light
a moment of pure being
no revels

still, the heart is full

ASCENT, DESCENT, NO MIDDLE GROUND

I say I would choose safety, I always say I want it, the steady
silent heartbeat, no heat, no cold, no spice, the air unremarkable,
just air, which is what I say I want *Please let me once be bored*
at least for a week, maybe more—

If I had to choose between this volcanic life and one that's safe,
always quiet, like a white room where no colors clash, or a
white noise with no discordant note—

I wouldn't choose a lifetime of never being hurried, never
knowing fear or exultation, passion or release or rage, never
knowing calm as a gift earned in chaos—

If I had to choose, I'd hush my prayer for peace and plunge
around the mountain, up, down, everywhere the path emerges,
into paintbrush, columbine, waterfall, snow.

Poems previously published:

"Flight from Detroit," *Sidewalks*
"From Room to Room," *Sing Heavenly Muse*
"His Mother Talks at Dinner," *North Country*
"No Language for This," *Dust and Fire: An Anthology of Women's Writing*
"One Prayer," *Mediphors*
"Past Pictures" as "Ohio Return," *Hurricane Alice*
"Two Chairs and an Umbrella Table," *Lynx Eye*
"The Woman Who Wailed," *Journey Notes*
"The Women," *Caprice*
"You Come Back," *A View from the Loft*
"Rogue River Run," *The Good Long Life*
"We Come Home," *Canadian Woman Studies*

About the Author

Elizabeth Bourque Johnson is a writer, a teacher, a mother, and a nurse. When her daughter died in a car accident, writing became a way to manage her grief. She earned an MA in creative writing and a PhD in literature at the University of Minnesota, where she has taught both writing and literature. Along the way, she developed a course called "Writing through Grief" offered through the Loft and the University of Minnesota's Compleat Scholar Program, and she speaks to grief groups throughout the Twin Cities.

In 2010 she co-edited and published with Ted Bowman *The Wind Blows, The Ice Breaks: Poems of Loss and Renewal by Minnesota Poets.*

Elizabeth's poetry has won local and national awards and has appeared in the literary press in the United States and Canada. She has also published scholarly articles in literature and in the health field.